WoS

ABERDEEN
CITY LIBRARIES
www.aberdeencity.gov.uk/libraries

Aberdeen City Cou...
Woodside Library
Tel. 484534

Return to ....
or any other Aberdeen City Library

Please return/renew this item by the last day shown. Items may also be renewed by phone or online

1 3 AUG 2012

03 OCT 12.

22. OCT 13.

06 JAN 14.

APR 15.

27. MAY 15

2 2 AUG 2015

11. OCT 16.

WITHDRAWN

Living with a
Houserabbit

Linda Dykes and Helen Flack

RINGPRESS

THE QUESTION OF GENDER
*The 'he' pronoun is used throughout this book in favour of the rather impersonal 'it',
but no gender bias is intended at all.*

ACKNOWLEDGEMENTS

The health chapters were written in consultation with Owen Davies BVSc, MRCVS.

636.9322

Published by Ringpress Books,
a division of Interpet Publishing,
Vincent Lane, Dorking, Surrey, RH4 3YX, UK
Tel: 01306 873822   Fax: 01306 876712

Series Director: Claire Horton-Bussey

Designed by Sarah Williams.

First Published 2003
© 2003 RINGPRESS BOOKS

ISBN 1 86054 207 7

Printed and bound in Singapore

0 9 8 7 6 5 4 3 2 1

CONTENTS

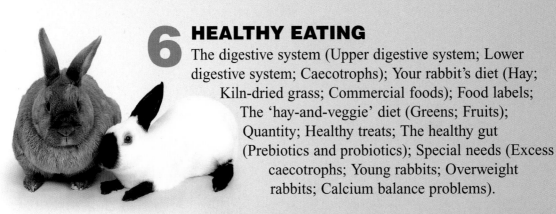

CHAPTER ONE

INTRODUCING THE HOUSERABBIT

What is a houserabbit? Well, quite simply, it is a rabbit that is kept indoors, in the family home, with freedom to move around, just like a cat or dog. Any pet rabbit can become a houserabbit, even one that has previously lived outdoors in a hutch. While some owners give their houserabbits a cage to live in when they're unsupervised, others allow their rabbits to be completely free-range, hopping about the home as they please.

You may be surprised to discover that keeping a bunny indoors isn't something new – it has been known for years that rabbits are easy to house-train! However, the traditional idea of the pet rabbit in a hutch, which dates back to Victorian times, is so established in our minds that many people are astonished when they first hear of rabbits happily roaming the family home and being successfully litter-trained.

It also comes as a surprise to many that houserabbits have a much better quality of life than rabbits confined to hutches at the bottom of the garden. Keeping any animal as a pet brings with it the responsibility of providing the animal with the environment and care that meets both its physical and behavioural needs. Sadly, life in caged, solitary confinement meets hardly any of the fundamental needs of the domestic rabbit, no more than would keeping a cat or dog in this way. The result is a bored and distressed pet.

WILD ORIGINS

Let's take a quick look at the lifestyle and natural habitat of the European wild rabbit, to explain why our domestic rabbits are so content living in the giant burrow that is a human home.

Domestic rabbits are the same species as the European wild rabbit, *Oryctolagus cuniculus*, which translates as "hare-like digger of underground passages". These fascinating animals evolved on the Iberian Peninsula (now Portugal and Spain). They have proved to be highly adaptable mammals, capable of thriving in habitats very different from those in which they originated.

Physical appearance

Our first glance at a rabbit reveals all the hallmarks of a prey animal, perfectly designed to

The rabbit's large, mobile ears act like radar dishes, ready to detect any sound of predators.

be on the lookout for, and to flee from, danger. Firstly, his large eyes provide a visual field of almost 360 degrees, to watch for predators. The rabbit is long-sighted and can see moving objects at a great distance. He is not so good at seeing things close up, having a blind spot directly in front of his nose.

Secondly, by swivelling their long ears around like radar dishes, rabbits are capable of tuning in to sounds from any direction. The rabbit's constantly twitching nose contains scent receptors, giving him a highly developed sense of smell.

Finally, our rabbit has large, powerful leg muscles. These combine with a lightweight skeleton, which enable him not only to sprint, but also to twist and turn with a remarkable degree of agility.

Behaviour

Physically, our rabbit is well designed for survival, but what about his behaviour? Rabbits are gregarious by nature, living in a large warren. This wild rabbit society is quite complex, with the community subdivided into smaller, hierarchical social groups, each of which is vying for territory. Rabbit behaviour varies from season to season. Territorial behaviour, and aggression fuelled by sex hormones, reach a peak at the height of the spring/summer breeding season and then ebb away to allow peaceful cohabitation in winter.

Warrens

In the rabbit's natural habitat, warrens are remarkable structures. They can be extensive, complex networks of interconnecting tunnels, sometimes constructed over decades and occupied by many consecutive generations of animals. Local soil conditions dictate the warren arrangements, with some rabbit colonies in very sandy areas not having proper warrens at all.

Female rabbits do most of the deep digging when constructing a warren. They use their front paws to dig and kick out the debris between their back legs. Every so often, the female will smooth out the earth in front of her with a pushing motion of the front paws. Any small plant roots hindering tunnel construction are dealt with by a swift nip; larger ones are gnawed away by continued effort!

Hygiene

Our rabbit will spend a large part of his time above ground simply feeding himself! He will also take the time to visit the communal latrine area. Like other animals that are born in nests, such as puppies and kittens, rabbits tend not to soil their living quarters. Wild rabbit communities use these communal latrines for most of their toilet needs, although some faecal droppings are scattered throughout the home range, a practice that has the additional benefit of helping to fertilise the grass that makes up the bulk of the diet.

Activity

While above ground, our rabbit may also indulge in play, leaping and frisking, practising the movements that may save him from a predator's grasp, or just sunning himself in a shallow, scraped-out hole. In general, however, rabbits retreat to the relative safety of their underground homes for about 16 hours out of every 24, sometimes more.

Feeding

Contrary to popular belief, rabbits are not nocturnal. They are crepuscular, which means they are most active at dawn and dusk. At these times, wild rabbits emerge from their burrows to feed, an activity that keeps them busy for around four hours every day. The bulk of the wild rabbit diet consists of grass.

To extract the maximum amount of goodness from grass, which is low in nutrients, rabbits, like many other herbivores, process grass in their digestive systems twice. Ruminants (goats and cows, etc.) chew the cud, but rabbits do things rather differently. Instead of regurgitating half-digested grass, rabbits allow their food to pass right the way through the digestive system before eating it for a second time.

In the large bowel, friendly bacteria ferment the grass, releasing the nutrients. This fermented grass emerges as soft, dark droppings called caecotrophs. These are then passed out of the anus and eaten by the rabbit, just as they are. Once food has passed through the gut a second time, all the nutrients have been extracted and the waste product is excreted as faecal droppings, which are the small, hard, raisin-like rabbit droppings with which we are familiar.

DOMESTICATION

Being placed at the bottom of the food chain makes for a hazardous life! Chief among the rabbit's predators is man.

Rabbits have been popular food for roughly 2,000 years, since man first hunted and trapped

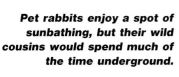

Pet rabbits enjoy a spot of sunbathing, but their wild cousins would spend much of the time underground.

Selective breeding led to the development of different rabbit breeds, such as the Dwarf Lop (left) and the Netherland Dwarf (right).

them for their meat and fur. Humankind soon found that there was an easier way to get rabbit meat – simply trap the animals and then let them breed in captivity.

Domestication of the rabbit began many years ago. We know that the Romans farmed rabbits for meat, initially keeping them in fenced enclosures alongside hares (which didn't work terribly well). This practice of fencing-in warrens was later continued by the Normans and lasted well into the Middle Ages. Escapes were inevitable, and the escapees bred like – well, like rabbits – quickly extending the rabbit population far beyond the shores of their native Iberian Peninsula!

The rabbits in these managed warrens retained their wild characteristics, and true domestication really began only when medieval monks started keeping rabbits in cages, to provide a readily

available food source for the monastery. Over time, and with selective breeding, these caged rabbits grew used to human company and they became tame.

Continued breeding from the same stock gave rise to spontaneous mutations in both coat type and colour. In captivity, away from the eyes of predators, these differently coloured rabbits survived.

Further selective breeding has resulted in a broadly diverse selection of coat and colour among domestic rabbits, so that there is a wide selection to choose from.

Breeding programmes

For many years, man's relationship with the rabbit continued to be one of convenience, with rabbits kept only for fur and for meat. However, things changed with the advent of the Industrial

Revolution. During this time, the human population migrated into towns and cities, and space for keeping livestock was severely limited. For country dwellers, used to keeping livestock to supplement the table, rabbits and pigeons became the only feasible option.

Over time, man's natural competitive instinct led to competitions to find the best-shaped, the best-coated, or the longest-eared rabbit, and so the rabbit fancy began. It led to selective breeding programmes, which established the forerunners of the breeds that we know now, such as lop-eared rabbits, giant breeds (often kept for meat, originally) and miniaturised breeds such as the Netherland Dwarf and the Polish.

The companion
By the 19th century, the appealing nature of rabbits resulted in their becoming established as pets as much as a supplement to the meat ration. Pet rabbits were known as 'sweethearts'. There are instances of indoor rabbits, mentioned as a curiosity, in books dating back to the late 18th century. The 18th-century poet, William Cowper, wrote about three tame hares he had living indoors, proving that not just rabbits, but also hand-reared hares, benefit from life inside the family home.

In the 1950s, a Dublin zookeeper, Cecil Webb, wrote a delightful book detailing his experiences of sharing his home with a hand-reared hare, to which he later added a companion rabbit.

Perhaps the most famous houserabbit to date belonged to Beatrix Potter. Her rabbit was the inspiration for the mischievous Peter Rabbit. Just like houserabbit owners today, Beatrix

found that sharing her home with a rabbit enabled far closer observation of character and behaviour than can ever be achieved observing a pet living in the garden. Her wonderful drawings of Peter and his family are the result of these observations. Other famous owners of indoor rabbits allegedly include Napoleon, who kept a bunny in prison with him, Louis XIV and Trotsky!

THE HUTCH RABBIT
Throughout the 20th century, keeping a rabbit in a hutch in the garden has been an integral part of many people's childhood. However, it is only in the past two decades that houserabbit keeping has really taken off. Today, rabbits are the third most popular pet in Britain, beaten only by cats and dogs. Hundreds of thousands of rabbits are sold in pet shops every year, but, sadly, the majority are still purchased as children's pets to live a conventional life in a hutch in the garden. Many people are still oblivious to the fact that they could enjoy their pet far more if they allowed him to live indoors as a houserabbit, which would also avoid a sad and lonely existence for the rabbit.

Perhaps one of the major reasons for this is that, until recently, routine neutering of pet

Life in a hutch – the common way that most rabbits spend their life.

rabbits was almost unheard of. Entire male rabbits – like entire tomcats – can make somewhat pungent housemates, and neutering is a real necessity for a life under the family roof. However, now that veterinary medicine has advanced sufficiently to allow safe, routine surgery on pet rabbits, there is no stopping the houserabbit movement.

THE HOUSE PET

The big breakthrough happened in the United States in the 1980s, when the Houserabbit Society was founded in 1989. Fuelled by the rapidly developing Internet, and subsequent ease of sharing information, interest in houserabbits spread worldwide.

The British Houserabbit Association was formed in 1996 (now incorporated into the Rabbit Welfare Association), and several other countries have now followed suit and formed their own houserabbit associations.

So, why are rabbits such appealing house pets?

Forming a relationship with an animal that would usually view you as a predator is deeply rewarding.

- First of all, rabbits are undeniably cute! They have immensely appealing faces, liquid eyes, and soft fur. They are also intelligent and responsive, capable of forming a very close bond with their owner.
- Secondly, houserabbits are practical pets to combine with a busy lifestyle. Many working people, who would struggle to find time to look after a dog or cat, are able to cope with a self-exercising, silent houserabbit. After all, rabbits don't bark, they don't need taking for walks, and you don't have to worry about them getting run over! Being crepuscular, rabbits are most active in the morning and evening, happy to rest for most of the day – this fits in beautifully with the working day.
- The third advantage is that, compared with

cats and dogs, the initial purchase price and ongoing maintenance expenses are far less for rabbits. There is no competition when it comes to the cost of feeding a rabbit compared to a Great Dane! However, veterinary costs for rabbits are little different from more traditional house pets. Rabbits need to be neutered and they must have annual vaccinations just like dogs and cats. Should your rabbit become ill, you may find yourself paying out hundreds of pounds in veterinary fees. Pet health insurance is now available for rabbits in the UK, and it is very strongly recommended.
- Finally, houserabbits are still scarce enough to be unusual; they make a guaranteed conversation piece at parties!

Perhaps the real reason for the growing

success of the houserabbit is that it is deeply satisfying to build a relationship with an animal that naturally regards you as a predator. Living alongside a bunny is an enriching experience, and, as time goes on and you gain your rabbit's trust, you will be rewarded with an amazing behavioural repertoire – a true insight into the private life of a uniquely private animal.

THE RABBIT'S REWARDS

It is easy to see that humans have much to gain from keeping rabbits as indoor pets. What, however, does the rabbit have to gain from this arrangement?

- A houserabbit will enjoy plenty of company from his human housemates. We have learned from the wild rabbit that company is important for the psychological wellbeing of this gregarious species. Of course, keeping a neutered pair of rabbits meets their need for company even better.
- A houserabbit gets more exercise. For an animal designed to spend several hours a day roaming a territory of many acres, life confined to a cage has harmful physical consequences and results in premature osteoporosis and painful spinal arthritis.

Houserabbits – even those kept in a cage when unsupervised – usually enjoy at least a couple of hours of freedom per day, and they are much fitter as a result.

- A houserabbit is noticed more. Kept traditionally in an outdoor hutch, a rabbit may have the attention of his owners for only a few minutes in every day, particularly in inclement weather. As prey animals, rabbits are programmed to conceal signs of illness, and, consequently, by the time a rabbit is showing obvious signs of discomfort, he may be gravely ill. The houserabbit, in contrast, spends several hours a day in the company of his or her owner. The slightest change in behaviour will attract immediate attention, and early veterinary advice can be sought. It is no coincidence that it is hutch rabbits who tend to 'die with no warning', not houserabbits.
- Throughout history, the rabbit has proved himself adaptable. He has thrived on several continents, coped with extremes of temperature and evolved into a domestic animal capable of interacting with his keepers. In nature, he lives in a complex social structure and survives against the odds in a world full of predators. For him, life inside a human house resembles one large and exciting burrow!

Hutch-rabbits get less attention and exercise than their lucky houserabbit counterparts, and are prone to developing skeletal problems.

CHAPTER TWO

IS A RABBIT FOR ME?

Taking on any pet is an important decision. You will need to look carefully at what you expect from your pet, as well as what you can offer in return. This is especially true with houserabbits. Most people have a fair idea what life with a dog or cat involves, but rabbits are very different from these traditional pets.

Kept correctly, the rabbit will be happy and will offer you years of pleasure. Getting it wrong means an unhappy situation for both you and the bunny. So, how will having a rabbit in the house affect you, your family, and your home?

HOUSE-SHARING

Houserabbits will live happily in just about any kind of human living space, from tiny flats to stately homes. However, it is important to consider the safety of the rabbit. How much of the house is going to be accessible to the bunny? Some areas, such as mezzanine levels that a rabbit could fall from, may need to be shut off – rabbits don't bounce!

You also need to decide if you are happy to accommodate a bunny's cage within your decor scheme. You will need a cage, at least temporarily, until your rabbit is fully trained, and some will need this option permanently. A large cage can take up a lot of space in a small house, and may look out of place among minimalist decor.

Bunny-proofing

As a houserabbit owner, you will also need to be prepared for your pet to inflict some wear and tear on your furnishings. While not in the same house-wrecking league as puppies, young rabbits in particular can be destructive. Stripped wallpaper, nibbled carpets, and damaged furniture are not uncommon, so it is advisable to start your bunny in a cage, supervising exercise time to minimise damage.

There will be plenty of time to build up to a free-range lifestyle when your rabbit has learned not to chew everything in sight. Even so, you will need to 'bunny-proof' your home to make sure it is safe for the rabbit. Starting off without a cage is not a good idea, unless you are willing to put up with significant mess and damage to the house.

Rabbits are very sociable animals and will enjoy the company of another bunny if you work during the day.

The house-proud

Like all pets, houserabbits are not for the obsessively house-proud. Rabbits will shed hair and sometimes drag a bit of hay on to the carpet. You will need to sweep or vacuum the rabbit living area daily.

If a bit of mess drives you up the wall, then an indoor bunny will cause you more stress than pleasure.

Allergies

Because of the amount of hair they shed, and the necessity to feed hay, rabbits may not be suitable pets for those who suffer from allergies. If you know you suffer from hay fever or other allergies, make sure you spend some time in close proximity to rabbits and hay before you decide to share your home with a houserabbit. Interestingly, some people who are allergic to cats are fine with rabbits.

Company

Caring for a pet rabbit will obviously take up some of your time. Houserabbits are quite happy to follow their natural behaviour patterns and rest during the day, but they will need company and stimulation in mornings and evenings to fit in with their crepuscular nature.

Unless you are around the house most evenings, your rabbit will be lonely. If you have less time to devote to a pet, and you are out for long periods during the day, consider taking on two rabbits – they will be much happier than one on his own.

COMMITMENT

Taking on a rabbit is a long-term commitment. You will have to care for him for the duration of his natural life – and rabbits can live a surprisingly long time. Seven to ten years is usual and, with advances in veterinary health care, teenage rabbits are not uncommon. While everyone's life has unexpected twists and turns, it is not fair to contemplate taking on a pet if you have no reasonable prospect of being able to look after him for the rest of his life.

Think through your circumstances and decide if you can reasonably expect to be in a position to care for a bunny in ten years time. If you are really keen to have a rabbit, but you think your lifestyle might undergo a major change in a few years, consider adopting an older rabbit or volunteering to be a foster carer, offering a safe haven for a succession of rescue rabbits on a temporary basis.

COSTS

In terms of cost, bunny 'running expenses' only amount to a few pounds or dollars per week. On the other hand, the initial costs of purchasing a cage and equipment can be quite high. Also to be considered are veterinary bills. It is distressing enough coping when your houserabbit is ill, without the added worry about a bill that could run to hundreds or even thousands of pounds or dollars. Pet health insurance is very strongly recommended to remove this worry. Even so, pet insurance does not cover routine, preventative health care, so you will still need to budget for neutering and for annual vaccinations.

OTHER PETS

If you already have other pets, you need to work out how a rabbit will fit in with the existing animal family (see Chapter Nine). Many people are initially attracted to houserabbits as an alternative to a dog or cat. Rabbits do make wonderful pets, but you must remember that a houserabbit is a rabbit, and not a small dog or cat. If you have previously lived with these species, you will need to mentally adjust your

Rabbits are not soft, cuddly toys – although they make great family pets, children should always be supervised when handling the animal.

expectations of your new pet, bearing in mind that a rabbit is a prey animal with very different behaviour patterns.

FAMILY LIFE

You need to be sure that everyone living in your home is keen to have a houserabbit and that they understand the restrictions this will put upon their lifestyles. For example, everyone will have to remember not to leave books on the floor as they will be nibbled, as well as always closing doors to non-bunny-proofed areas.

Holiday arrangements will be more restricted. You will have to arrange care for the bunny in advance, which might put an end to impulsive trips away from home.

If you have children, ask yourself carefully why you want a rabbit. If you are looking for a cuddly pet that the kids can look after as a lesson in responsibility, please think again.

Rabbits really aren't very good children's pets. They can make wonderful family pets, but only if adults accept the responsibility for the rabbit and all his care. You should remember that a houserabbit is not a toy – he has the same needs as any other living animal.

Successfully mixing rabbits and children involves teaching the children responsibility and restraint. For example, they should only interact with the rabbit at ground level, and only when the bunny initiates play.

This can be a difficult lesson for young children to grasp. They will naturally want to hold their pet, but allowing children to pick up a rabbit so often leads to disaster. Rabbits will kick, scratch and bite if they feel at all insecure, and many rabbits die from spinal injuries after being dropped by children.

Integrating the rabbit's needs with teaching acceptable behaviour to the children is hard work, but a houserabbit will repay this by interacting confidently with the kids.

Older people, and those with physical disabilities, are often attracted to houserabbits. There are many success stories where they have proved to be the perfect companion.

However, you must ascertain whether you can cope physically with the care a rabbit needs. For example, picking up the rabbit to clip claws can be very difficult for people with limited strength and mobility in their hands. Alternatively, you could arrange for assistance with your new pet before you bring him home.

LIVING ARRANGEMENTS

Outdoor runs

Many houserabbits spend all their time indoors. This is not a problem as long as the rabbit has plenty of space, environmental enrichment, and company. However, if you have a garden, there's no doubt that most houserabbits really enjoy the opportunity to run and play outside.

Allowing your rabbit access to the garden poses hazards both to the rabbit and to the garden. Neighbourhood cats, dogs, and foxes are a real threat to domestic rabbits and many garden plants are potentially toxic. Your rabbit is also capable of inflicting considerable damage on your garden. He will dig in the lawn and borders, behead flowers, and nibble plant roots. A rabbit can demolish the handiwork of a keen gardener in a matter of hours. Unless you are able to stay outdoors and supervise every garden play session, the safest option is to purchase or build a spacious outdoor lawn-run. The ideal lawn-run is easy to move and sturdily built to prevent attack by predators. It should have a covered area or a space in which to place a hutch. If your rabbit is likely to spend long periods unsupervised in the run, cover the

A lawn-run will be enjoyed by your rabbit, and is the only safe option if you are unable to supervise him outdoors.

bottom of the run with wire mesh as well. The grass will poke through for your rabbit to nibble, but he won't be able to dig his way out. Lawn-runs sold in pet shops are often rather flimsy. A better option is a chicken run, or one made by a specialist joinery company.

Half-and-half lifestyles

If you wish to keep your rabbit partly indoors and partly outside, there are various options to consider. Most owners allow their rabbits to spend the daytime out in their lawn-run and evenings and night in the house. If there is constant access to a dry, cosy shelter, this routine can continue all year round, regardless of the weather. Bunnies kept like this grow a thick winter coat, and relish being outside even when the weather is terrible. There's no doubt that rabbits are perfectly happy with this lifestyle.

However, it is worth considering the abrupt changes of temperature involved, especially during the winter. You will need to ensure that your rabbit's overnight accommodation is cooler than the rest of the house. What you must not do is keep the bunny in your heated home during the day and then return him to a cold outdoor hutch at night during the winter.

Another possibility is where the rabbit lives outdoors in the warmer months of the year but moves indoors full-time once the weather turns colder. This works well too, but you may have to reintroduce the litter tray formally each time.

Come inside

If you have an outdoor rabbit that you would like to have living indoors as a houserabbit, it's best to start off in spring. Bringing in an outdoor rabbit in the middle of winter is not advised because your rabbit will immediately go into a heavy moult and grow a thinner coat. If you then decide not to proceed, he'll be too cold

A sheltered outdoor hutch with a safe exercise area can be used during the summer months

if you put him outside again. If you introduce the rabbit to life indoors in spring and things don't work out, he'll be able to resume outdoor life while the weather is still warm.

Finally, training houserabbits to use a cat-flap, so that they have free access to the garden, is not recommended. Your bunny would be at very real risk of becoming a quick snack for an urban fox.

YOUR CHOICE

Before you choose your houserabbit, it is worth doing some research into what kind of rabbit you would like. There's a huge range of breeds to choose from, as well as an unlimited number of delightful crossbreeds. Pet shops will have a very limited choice, so, to get an idea of what is available, try visiting a rabbit show, buying a

FIRST BUNNY LOVE

Sally Stevens got her first houserabbit shortly after buying her first house. She works as cabin crew for a major airline and finds that a houserabbit suits her lifestyle very well.

"I've always loved animals, but living in rented accommodation for years meant that I couldn't have a pet. When I finally managed to buy my little house, I was determined to change this and was thinking about adopting a rescue cat. My work sometimes takes me away from home overnight and I work very irregular hours, so a dog was out of the question, and I thought that a cat would be more independent. However, although I like cats, I wasn't entirely sure if that was what I wanted – they sometimes seem rather aloof and I knew I would worry about a cat being run over.

"One Sunday afternoon, I was looking around a garden centre with my boyfriend, when we saw these rabbits for sale. One of them was a little black bunny with one floppy ear and one straight ear. She hopped over to the edge of the pen and seemed to say hello! Years before this, I had laughed at a colleague for phoning home from Greece to check how her pet rabbit was. She had explained that it was a special, house-trained rabbit who lived indoors, so I knew it was possible to train rabbits. Why shouldn't I have a rabbit as a pet? We bought the rabbit and Loppie, as she became known, came home with me.

"This was all a while ago, before there was any information available about houserabbits, so we learnt as we went along. Loppie was delightful and soon trained to use a litter tray, the only problem being that it had to be placed on my front doormat, as that was where she went to the loo! It took ages to persuade her to go elsewhere.

"Most of the time, Loppie lived in a wooden rabbit hutch in my front room. It looked a bit odd, but it doubled as a small table once I put a wooden top on it. I used to let her out to run around the house whenever I was at home.

"I did feel guilty about leaving her caged when I was at work, but I'd had lots of accidents with the house. She cut off my phone mid-call on one occasion, because I hadn't protected the cable! She also badly damaged my carpets behind the sofa where she loved to dig. I definitely wouldn't recommend a rabbit for anyone who has spent a fortune on interior decor.

"Looking after Loppie, however, was very easy. The cage just needed sweeping out and the litter tray changing each day. She needed fresh food and water every morning, so, whenever I was away overnight, my next-door neighbour kindly popped in to see to Loppie.

"By the time she was two years old, she was much better behaved and I could leave her out all the time. It was about this time that I decided it wasn't fair to leave her on her own and decided to get her a companion. But that's another story…"

Loppie soon made herself at home in Sally's house.

book, or looking on the Internet. While every rabbit is unique, it is possible to make some generalisations about the characteristics of the different breeds.

Size

Rabbits range in size from tiny, dwarf breeds, such as the Netherland Dwarf and the Polish, which weigh around 1 kg (2 to 2.5 lbs), to giants like the French Lop, the Vlaamse Reus, and the British Giant, which may exceed 8 kg (18.2 lbs). Between these extremes are breeds of every size. Crossbreeds tend towards the middle of the weight range.

The size of the rabbit you choose is actually quite important. Generally, the smaller the rabbit, the more lively he is likely to be and the longer he is likely to live. It is more difficult to 'bunny-proof' against the inquisitive dwarf breeds, as they are small enough to slip behind the washing machine or into other attractive nooks and crannies around the house. Larger breeds tend to be more placid, and, some would argue, they make better house pets. However, longevity is a problem in the giant breeds, which may live for three to four years only. The reason for this is not yet clear.

If you have children, dogs or cats, it would be wise to choose a larger bunny. Many people assume that a dwarf breed would be better for a child to handle, but, as we've already discussed, this is not recommended. The bigger the rabbit, the better; young children will be less inclined to try to pick him up. Similarly, a cat that hunts young, wild rabbits will think twice before picking a fight with a bunny larger than herself!

From a small Dwarf Lionhead (top) to a huge French Lop (bottom), there is a rabbit to suit most preferences and lifestyles.

Ears

You have probably noticed that some rabbits have upright ears while others have ears that flop down. These lop-eared breeds are currently the most popular pet rabbits, mainly because this is the type of rabbit most often sold in pet shops.

Lops come in a whole range of sizes. The smallest are the Miniature Lops, weighing around 1.5 kg (3.5 lbs), while the largest are the massive French Lops. In between these two ends of the scale are the Dwarf Lop, at around 2 kg (4.6 lbs), the slightly larger German Lop, and the Cashmere Lop, a long-haired variant of the Dwarf Lop. The rare English Lop has ears so long they trail on the ground, and the final member of the Lop family, the Meissner, is the rarest of them all.

Lops tend to be happy, outgoing rabbits who do well as pets. However, the popular Dwarf and Miniature Lops are at higher risk of dental and eye disease. With these breeds, it is very important to know what you are buying. Go to a reputable breeder whose rabbits have no history of teeth problems, or adopt an adult rescue rabbit whose teeth have been checked at the time of neutering. Beware of buying from a pet shop, where you have no information about the rabbit's history.

Age

Baby rabbits are undeniably cute, but it's a misconception to believe that they will be easier to train than an older animal. Young rabbits are very hard work. It's great fun watching them grow, but they get up to all sorts of mischief and can be remarkably destructive.

By the time a rabbit reaches his first birthday, he should be calming down a bit. He may be neutered already (if he is not, he will be old enough to be neutered immediately), and he should have grown out of his most destructive phase. He'll be a bit less distractible, and, therefore, easier to litter-train.

Most importantly, you can really assess the character of an adult rabbit. Baby rabbits are a lottery in terms of temperament and character, unless you know the parents. Even with careful and regular handling, adorable young bunnies can still grow into rabbits who prefer not to have close interaction with their owners. Overall, a rabbit at least a year old is a much better prospect for the novice houserabbit owner.

Coat type

There are three basic coat types: normal, rex and long-haired. Normal-coated rabbits range from the thin, shiny coat of the Polish, Silver or Tan, to the thicker, softer fur of the Lops and traditional fur breeds. Rex rabbits have no guard hairs, and their beautiful coat feels and looks like velvet. Long-haired breeds include the Angora and the Cashmere Lop, and semi-longhaired animals like the Lionhead have recently become available.

You should only contemplate a long-haired rabbit if you are willing to spend several hours a week grooming him, or if you are prepared to clip the coat every few weeks. Otherwise, these beautiful but vulnerable rabbits end up as a miserable matted mess. Even Lionheads will need extra attention, as their long ruff extends under the chin, where rabbits are particularly likely to mat.

Thick-coated rabbits often moult heavily when kept indoors, and keeping up with the vast quantities of hair being shed at these times can be quite a task. Lighter-coated or Rex rabbits are much easier on the vacuum cleaner.

FINDING YOUR RABBIT

Unless you have your heart set on a particular breed or colour, please consider adopting a

LOP VARIETIES

The Dwarf Lop is a smaller, more manageable size than his larger relatives.

The Cashmere Lop: a long-haired variant of the Dwarf Lop.

The English Lop's huge ears trail on the ground.

The Meissner: the rarest of all Lops.

The Lop Lionhead requires extra grooming around the head area.

The French Lop: a huge breed with a teddy bear face.

COAT TYPE

The 'normal' coat ranges from the soft, thick coat (left), to the shiny, thin coat of a Polish (right).

Rex: a velvety, luxurious coat.

Semi-longhaired: the ruff of this Lionhead will need special attention.

The long-haired coat of a Cashmere (left) and an Angora (right) requires considerable grooming.

rescue rabbit. Tens of thousands of rabbits, of all breeds, ages, and sizes, end up in rescue centres every year through no fault of their own. Increasingly, rescue rabbits are put up for adoption only when they have been neutered and vaccinated, which means that you can adopt a rabbit all ready for a new start as your housebunny.

If you are keen to share your life with a pedigree rabbit, you will need to find a reputable breeder. Older animals are often offered for sale when they are no longer required as part of a breeding programme. This can be a way of offering a loving home to a well-handled rabbit who may otherwise have an uncertain future.

Always visit the breeder and ensure you are satisfied with the conditions in which the rabbits are kept. Most show rabbits live in hutches stacked in several tiers, but they should have plenty of room and the hutches should be kept clean.

Buying a baby rabbit from a pet shop often seems the convenient option. Unfortunately, many baby rabbits sold by retail outlets have been bred in factory-farm conditions, with little or no early socialisation with people. Furthermore, as they will have to endure two

A rescued rabbit can make a perfect companion.

changes of environment in quick succession, they are at a higher risk of serious – possibly even fatal – digestive upsets than rabbits from rescue or from a breeder.

CHAPTER THREE

PREPARING FOR YOUR HOUSERABBIT

Before welcoming your rabbit into your home, there are a number of preparations to make. The first step is to bunny-proof all the areas to which the rabbit will have access. This is vital, otherwise you will be amazed by the talent your new pet shows as a horticulturist, electrician, wood carver and interior designer! There are few houserabbit-owning households who have not, at some point, had their telephone cable savaged by the rabbit.

However, bunny-proofing isn't needed only to protect your furnishings from your rabbit; it is necessary to protect your rabbit from your home, which is a potentially hazardous environment for a rabbit. Rabbits can squeeze into tiny spaces, climb to remarkable heights, and show a dogged determination when it comes to accessing forbidden areas. They have a natural urge to dig and chew. You will need to be alert and determined to prevent damage.

BUNNY-PROOFING

Follow this simple bunny-proofing guide to stay one step ahead of your rabbit – and remember,

always be suspicious if he goes quiet while hidden behind furniture.

- **Prevent access.** The simplest way to bunny-proof places containing lots of cables, such as the back of the television or the computer, is to prevent access to them. Block off the area completely and shorten any dangling cables. Beware of any small dark holes. It is very difficult to extract a baby bunny from behind the washing machine or fridge!
- **Prevent damage.** If you can't block off an area, take steps to ensure that the rabbit can't cause any damage – covering any remaining cables (see below), for example.
- **Provide alternatives.** Offer attractive toys to your bunny. He will be less likely to pursue the forbidden alternatives.
- **Supervise.** Watch your rabbit while he is out and about. Occasional teeth marks are to be expected, but wholesale destruction indicates that your rabbit is not yet ready for unlimited freedom.

Cables and wires

Wild rabbits chomp readily through any plant

roots encountered when they are digging, and, to your houserabbit, power cables and telephone wires look just like plant roots. Shorten any dangling cables, fix longer cables just above the skirting board, and consider covering them with commercial conduit. If it doesn't dangle, it's much less attractive to the bunny.

Wires can also be covered with plastic water piping, slit lengthways and wrapped around the wire. Make use of commercial cable tidies to reduce the number of dangling wires behind household appliances. If you are a competent electrician, consider turning your electrical sockets the other way up – no more dangling cable – and fitting a circuit breaker to your household electrical supply. However well behaved your rabbit, never risk leaving power cables unprotected.

Houseplants
It is best to move all plants out of reach. Houseplants are often poisonous, and, therefore, dangerous. Even if you find harmless plants, your rabbit is likely to ruin them by munching their leaves or digging in the pot. You can protect the trunk of large plants by cutting out a cardboard circle and placing this over the soil in the pot.

Wallpaper
There is a very good reason why many houserabbit owners favour paint effects rather than wallpaper. Rabbits love to tug at even the tiniest piece of loose paper and many will hone in on textured paper with a vengeance. Some are real pros, stripping all the paper from the lower part of the wall.

If you are not yet ready to part with your wallpaper, you can try fixing clear perspex panels at least 30 cm (1 ft) high above the skirting boards. Alternatively, you could put something

slippery (perspex or a clear plastic carpet protector) on the floor of favourite wallpaper-tugging locations, to prevent the rabbit getting any purchase with his feet while tugging.

Soft furnishings
Digging is natural behaviour for bunnies, and, once they start to tug at carpets, it can be very difficult to discourage them. Room corners are particularly vulnerable. Prevent damage to the carpet by putting a triangle of perspex over the area.

You must also provide a safe outlet for digging behaviour. Carpet squares, or doormats made of natural materials such as seagrass and

Carpet-chewing is a favourite past-time of houserabbits.

A wooden floor is the best option, although your rabbit will need time to adjust to the more slippery surface.

coir, can be put in room corners and the rabbit encouraged to dig in these areas.

Solid floors, such as wood, laminates and vinyls, require no bunny-proofing. Once your rabbit has learned to hop on the slippery surface, they are probably the best option as they are so easy to clean.

You may need to shorten your curtains before your rabbit does the job for you, with a delightful scalloped effect. You can try using hold-ups, or simply tie the curtain up above bunny level when the rabbit is out roaming. Draw up blinds when your rabbit is in the room and keep the cords out of his way, both to prevent them from being nibbled, and also for the safety of your bunny; there is a known case of a rabbit being strangled in the cord of a floor-length blind.

Furniture
Any furniture is vulnerable to bunny attack, especially if the rabbit can squeeze under or behind it. Either block up the gaps or deliberately equip the area as a bunny playground. For example, the gap between a

sofa and a wall is the perfect place to put a tunnel made from a large-bore plastic drainage pipe. Alternatively, you could use a roll of off-cut carpet (carpet side in) to make a tunnel where your rabbit can burrow to his heart's content.

THE HOUSERABBIT HOME
Your rabbit will need a base in your house that he can call home. Your ultimate goal may be to have a rabbit who is free to choose where he sleeps; a rabbit who runs to the front door to greet you when you come home. However, this won't happen overnight. Until your rabbit is reliably trained, it is best to use a cage. This may be a disappointment if you hate the idea of caged animals, but the confinement should only be temporary and is a step along the way to complete freedom. If you elect to start without a cage, be prepared for high levels of supervision, a great deal of tolerance, and a lot of mess.

Curtains should be shortened – or your rabbit will do the job for you!

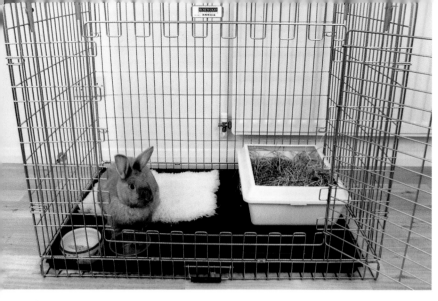

The indoor home should be spacious and secure.

As wild rabbits spend two-thirds of their time underground in very cramped burrows, your rabbit will be quite content in a roomy cage overnight or when you are at work, providing he can come out for several hours every day. You can then build up his freedom gradually, without sacrificing your home.

The cage
The cage should be spacious and comfortable. It should be easy to clean and look good in your living room. You can buy indoor rabbit cages that look like giant hamster cages, with a deep plastic tray clipped to a wire top. While these are more than adequate, they tend to occupy a lot of floor space.

Traditional wooden hutches can be used indoors, and they can be painted to match your decor. You'll need to seal the wood with non-toxic varnish or gloss paint, to prevent urine soaking into the wood and causing a bad smell.

There are companies making houserabbit cages that look like expensive pine furniture and which double as coffee tables – very chic!

Fold-up dog cages make versatile houserabbit homes. These sturdy wire cages have a shallow, plastic inner tray and fold up to suitcase size when not in use, making them easy to transport and to store. Various sizes are available, a 21- x 24- x 27-inch (52.5- x 60- x 67.5- cm) version will make a comfy home for a medium-sized rabbit who is given plenty of free-running time each day. Pet shops stock these cages but they are often cheaper when purchased by mail order from specialist outlets aimed at dog exhibitors.

As an alternative to a cage, you could fence off a small area in a room with an easy-clean floor. Some people use a utility room or porch, but there is a risk that your rabbit will not learn to integrate into your family.

Cage furniture
Furnish the cage with a bed, a litter tray, and food and water bowls. To make a perfect bed, cut a peep-hole in the side of a cardboard box and line it with an old cotton towel or a piece of fleecy veterinary bedding.

Cat litter trays are suitable for rabbits. Big rabbits need surprisingly large trays to prevent them from urinating over the side. If your rabbit has an accident just outside the tray, you'll need to get one with higher sides or a detachable rim. Corner litter trays are available, but even the large size is a squash for most rabbits and many people with large bunnies find alternatives, such as potting trays.

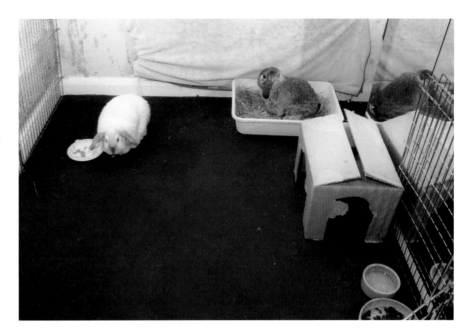

A large puppy pen can be adapted to convert part of a room into a bunny zone.

You will also need a couple of ceramic food bowls, and a water bottle or bowl. Rabbits will pick up and toss around lightweight food and water bowls, so the best option are the 5-inch (12.5-cm) ceramic bowls sold in most pet shops.

Most rabbits prefer drinking from a bowl. Water bottles tend to drip and can become blocked. It is not unknown for a rabbit to stop eating because he is thirsty, simply due to a blocked water bottle. If you use a bottle, choose one with a ball-bearing in the spout, and check it regularly to ensure that it has not become blocked and that the water is free-flowing.

Line the cage floor with newspaper. Put about one inch (2.5 cms) of cat litter in the litter tray, and top up by adding a good handful of hay. Then you're all set for the arrival of your new houserabbit.

CHAPTER FOUR

THE FIRST DAYS

Before collecting your rabbit, set up the cage in a quiet, bunny-proofed room. The living room is usually the best place, but, if you have a hectic household with children, make sure your rabbit cage is not in the middle of a paediatric racetrack.

If you know what your rabbit has been fed on, you should have bought in supplies. If not, make sure the breeder or rescue organisation gives you some of his usual food.

COLLECTING YOUR RABBIT

Take a suitable container with you when you collect your rabbit. A sturdy cardboard box lined with newspaper is adequate for very short journeys, but it's better to buy a suitable small-animal carrier. Try to choose one with an opening top.

Do not try to bring your rabbit home on your lap. He will be much happier travelling in a private 'surrogate burrow'.

The day you bring home your new houserabbit will be an exciting one for you, but for him the experience will be unsettling. He will have to get used to new sights, sounds and smells. He will need to learn your routine, and, if he is a baby, to cope without his littermates. During this confusing time, his instinct will tell him to hide down a burrow, just like a wild rabbit!

THE HOMECOMING

Once you get home, put your rabbit into his cage and leave him alone. What your rabbit needs during his first days in your home is peace and quiet.

Despite this, rabbits have an overwhelming curiosity, and yours will soon begin to interact with you, his new carer. At this stage, however, everything should be initiated by the rabbit. Building a trusting relationship will take time, and you must resist the temptation to pick up and cuddle your new pet. To a rabbit, this is the action of a predator, not a protector.

Children find this particularly difficult to grasp, and you will have to ensure that everyone realises that interactions with the new bunny are 'hands off' for the time being. Your bunny's cage should be somewhere he can gain access to easily, where he can relax in peace. It is essential that your rabbit feels safe inside his cage. Do not pester your rabbit when he is in his cage. You may have to gently pop your rabbit into his carrying box while you attend to cleaning his cage, but don't pick him up and hold him for prolonged cuddles.

LITTER-TRAINING

Your rabbit will start to learn to use his litter tray in the first few days. Rabbits are naturally clean animals and will tend to urinate in the same place. When you collect your rabbit, bring some soiled bedding with you and pop it into the new litter tray. As it will smell the same, he should go to the tray the next time he needs to wee. If he makes a mistake outside his tray, move the soiled piece of newspaper into the litter tray.

Because rabbits use droppings as social and territorial marking, persuading your rabbit to leave his droppings in the tray may be more difficult. Making his cage very much his own territory will help. Rabbits also tend to deposit droppings while munching hay, so cover the litter with hay and try hiding edible treats in the litter box to encourage him to frequent it more.

After a quiet settling-in period, make friends with the rabbit by hand-feeding him treats in the cage.

BECOMING FRIENDS

Over the next 24 to 48 hours, you can start to sit near the cage and talk to your bunny. If he comes up to the wire, you can scratch his nose and talk to him. Edible bribes are a perfectly acceptable way to make friends.

After a few days, he should be more relaxed and using his litter tray fairly well. Now it's time to start letting him out of the cage. Choose a time when there is not too much activity going on and you have a good half an hour free of distraction in order to supervise your rabbit. It is best to let out your rabbit just before feeding time, so that he has an extra incentive to go home when you want him to; he is also less likely to mess before food.

Open the door and let your rabbit venture out in his own time. He may hop out immediately or he may take a while to pluck up

With time and patience, your houserabbit will soon learn to be house-trained.

When he is brave enough to venture outside his cage, lie on the floor and reward him with treats when he approaches you.

enough courage to leave the safety of his cage. Lie on the floor, with a good supply of the treats, and, if he comes near you, talk to him and offer him a treat. If he lets you, you can rub his nose, but don't grab at him and don't pick him up.

If you see him raising his tail and about to urinate somewhere he shouldn't, either clap your hands or stamp your foot and say "No!" He'll stop immediately (your actions will startle him), but you know he needs to go and it's time he went home – 10 to 15 minutes is more than long enough for his first out-of-cage experience.

BEDTIME

To get your rabbit back to his cage, fill his food bowl, rattle it loudly, and put it inside. Hopefully, he will head back in the direction of the cage. If he doesn't, you'll have to herd him back in. It's vital he goes back into the cage under his own steam. The easiest way is to shepherd him gently back to his cage, clapping your hands and saying "Go home" or "Bedtime".

Most rabbits will happily hop back into their cage, but, if yours is a bit reluctant, arrange the furniture to make a corridor leading to the door. This will leave your rabbit no option but to hop back home. When he's in there, immediately praise him and offer him a treat so that he learns that going home means a treat. He will soon be whizzing back to his cage ready for his treat when you tell him to go home.

Practise this at least once every day, preferably more. Older rabbits can sometimes come out for fairly long periods straightaway, while babies should start with much shorter sessions. Most rabbits will happily go in and out of their cage during their free-running time, because, to them, it is their home, not a prison. They might pop back in to visit their litter tray, or to have a drink or a snack. That's wonderful behaviour!

TOO MUCH FREEDOM

Houserabbit owner Alan Best, from Kent, describes the domestic devastation caused by his rabbit, Daisy, when she was initially allowed too much freedom.

"Our first rabbit had a maloccluded jaw, which meant she couldn't chew anything. At worst, she could suck on the furniture. How unprepared we were then for Daisy, a six-month-old, unneutered female Dutch, with all her dental armoury intact and in full working order. She had been cooped up for all her short life, so we wanted to give her the full freedom she deserved.

"What a good idea it seemed to give her the run of the house. What a good idea to give her access to the back of the rather expensive sofa we purchased, just like a rabbit burrow. Perhaps not! Daisy behaved like a child who had just been given the keys to the sweet shop. Behaving naturally like any burrowing animal, Daisy shredded the sofa, severed wires (somehow avoiding electrocution), tore up the corners of the carpet (managing to avoid lacerating her paws on the carpet grippers), and generally had the time of her life, completely oblivious to the screams of her human companions.

"We were at our wits' end. It's surprising how quickly you can lose it with one, small furry creature! Someone said 'she will improve when she's neutered'. It was all quiet for a day or so after

Alan Best with Daisy the teenager from hell (left) and Gilbert (right).

the operation, then it was business as usual.

"Joining the British Houserabbit Association brought advice and light at the end of the tunnel. First the bad news – she was going through the teenage 'rabbit-from-hell' phase and this behaviour might take 18 months to settle down. The good news was that there was something we could do to help her and us.

"We provided Daisy with plenty of distractions – toys to throw, wood to chew, boxes to scrape. We bunny-proofed the house by removing wires from reach, protecting corners of carpets, defending skirting boards.

"Importantly, we limited Daisy's horizons to a more confined part of the house for a time, extending them gradually. Good, sound advice, ignored at our peril.

"So, our human house was converted into a rabbit shanty town of cardboard boxes and carpet samples, and Daisy was confined to whatever room we were in at the time. The kitchen became base camp.

"A dramatic influence on Daisy's behaviour was the recommendation from our vet to change her diet from pre-prepared dried food to hay and grass. Almost at once, Daisy turned her attentions away from soft furnishings. Why? One expert said that rabbits have a need for low-grade fibre – so it's either hay and grass, or your wallpaper and carpet. You take your choice! Another said it's because a bunny spending all day eating does not have the time to wreck your house. Either way, who cares? It helped us, even if it does not work for everyone, and the bunny will be the better for it (although the hay gets everywhere – even in your bed!).

"And what about Daisy? She's three now and has a soulmate, Gilbert. Life is about sleeping and eating and she has the run of the place. Lessons have been learned and we are beginning to reap the fruits of our labour. Daisy lets us know that, every so often (when we drop our guard), she may have grown up now, but she's still a teenager at heart.

"Just one final bit of advice… Forget your need for material possessions and your aspirations to be house-proud. Rabbits are great levellers of such thoughts. Remember this, and your life with a houserabbit will be a mutually rewarding experience – honestly!"

HEALTH CHECKS

Once your rabbit will come to you for treats, it is time to start training him to accept being picked up for routine health checks. Pick him up just for a moment or two, and, if he doesn't struggle, set him down again and immediately reward him. Gradually build up the time you hold him, and practise checking his nose, teeth, and bottom.

From this stage, you can work towards building a good bond with your rabbit. Gradually increase his free-running time, and, perhaps, progress towards allowing him access to a larger selection of bunny-proofed rooms.

Training your houserabbit to 'go home' on command is a very useful – and simple – exercise.

CHAPTER FIVE

CARING FOR YOUR HOUSERABBIT

R outine care of your houserabbit is simple and straightforward. Incorporate the following basic strategies into your routine and your rabbit should stay healthy and happy. It may seem a lot to start with, but you will quickly develop your own, time-efficient regime.

EVERY DAY

Your rabbit will need food, water, company and exercise every day, and it is your responsibility to provide them. You should also perform a basic, daily health check, so that any problems can be identified and dealt with promptly.

Nutrition

If you can, feed your rabbit twice a day at a regular time. Once he has settled in, you will probably find he starts begging when he thinks a meal is due. Even though rabbits should have access to hay at all times, they still look forward to their mealtimes, when they are fed their mix, pellets, or a pile of vegetables.

The behaviour of your rabbit at feeding time is a valuable indicator of his general health. If a greedy rabbit loses his enthusiasm for food, you know something is wrong. Feeding twice a day doubles the opportunities to observe your rabbit's appetite and his feeding pattern. You should also refresh the water in his bowl or bottle on a daily basis.

Exercise

Until your rabbit has been trained enough to be left unsupervised in a room (or, later on, in the whole house), he will spend most of his time in his cage.

You must ensure that he has at least two exercise periods a day, aiming for a minimum of two to four hours free-running time per day in the first few weeks.

Most people let their rabbit out of the cage as soon as they get up in the morning, popping him back in with the bribe of his breakfast. When you return from work, he can come out a second time, to spend the evening with you. Free-range houserabbits will choose how and when they want to exercise themselves.

Set some quality time aside each day to spend with your houserabbit.

Company

There is not much point in having a pet unless you spend some time enjoying his company. Set aside some time every day to spend with your rabbit. At first, his time out of the cage will be spent with you training him. However, he also needs to get to know you as a companion and as a source of fun.

Try sitting or lying on the floor to read a book, or to watch television. Even shy rabbits are usually overcome by curiosity and will eventually sneak up on you, possibly jumping on your back or lap. Keep a supply of edible treats with you and he will soon learn to come to you when you call his name. If your rabbit chooses to snuggle up beside you, to sit on your lap, or to groom your hair, he is paying you a big compliment. It is always best if he initiates contact – don't scare him off by constantly trying to cuddle him.

As his confidence grows, so your rabbit will initiate more and more contact with you.

Your bunny will soon gain confidence and explore all the furniture, including your bed or sofa. It is probably not a good idea to allow your rabbit on the bed and sofa until he is completely litter-trained. Urinating on sofas and beds is a common problem and it is not a habit you want to encourage.

Many rabbits like to sleep on beds and sofas. It's entirely up to you whether or not you let your furry companion share your bed with you at night, but, if you do, be aware of the drawbacks. Bunnies make great hot water bottles, but, should they decide that you are in their way, they will nip you to make you move. This is what they would do to other rabbits.

Even if you are not allergic to rabbits, overnight exposure to rabbit fur can be too much for some people to tolerate. Finally, consider the reaction of your human partner before allowing your rabbit nocturnal access to the bedroom.

Regular health checks will get your rabbit accustomed to being handled and will alert you to any early signs of ill health.

Health checks

Pick up your rabbit briefly to check him over. Reward him with a treat when you have finished, so that he will learn to accept this routine handling. Keep a lookout for runny eyes, nasal discharge, and a dirty bottom, all of which are signs of ill health.

If your rabbit is pedigree, he may be fitted with a metal identification ring on his hind leg. Check this daily, to ensure it is not too tight. Have it cut off next time your rabbit has an anaesthetic for any reason.

Next, check the litter tray. There should be roughly the same number and size of droppings every day. Monitor how much your rabbit eats and drinks. Be alert to any reduction in appetite,

or a change in his favourite foods. Any drastic change in water consumption should also be investigated.

It is normal to find occasional caecotrophs in the litter tray (or on the carpet, in which case leave them to dry before scraping them off). These are special droppings, normally eaten by the rabbit directly after they are expelled from the anus (see Chapter One). They look like tiny bunches of grapes, usually dark in colour, slightly shiny, and strong-smelling. If they appear regularly in his tray, or if they stick to his bottom, have your bunny checked by the veterinarian.

EVERY FEW DAYS

Cleaning bowls

Scrub food and water bowls two or three times a week, taking care to rinse them in fresh water to remove all traces of detergent.

Litter tray

Your rabbit's litter tray will need cleaning once or twice a week. Be careful not to overclean it. If you clean the litter tray too often, the rabbit may not recognise the smell as the toilet he has

The litter tray needs cleaning once or twice a week.

become accustomed to, and he will be less inclined to go again in the same place. Also, if you change the position of the litter tray, or the kind of litter you use, you may inadvertently confuse your rabbit and cause him to choose his own alternative loo.

If your rabbit tends to use one end of the tray, use a small shovel to remove the soiled litter from the 'dirty' end every two to three days.

Push the unused litter to that end, and refill with fresh litter. This will preserve the scent for the bunny but keep the tray odour-free for you.

If your rabbit revels in messing up his whole litter tray, you will need to replace all the litter two to three times a week. If you do this, keep back a small amount of soiled litter and put it on top of the fresh litter.

It is best to use a good-quality substrate, such as cat litter, to absorb urine in the litter tray. Rabbits produce a relatively large quantity of urine, so newspaper or kitchen towel will need changing frequently. If you use paper, you may find that urine will splash back on to the rabbit, and you will end up with a rabbit conditioned to urinate on any newspapers left lying on the floor – including the one you were reading!

Hay

Whatever substrate you choose, put a good handful of hay or straw on the top. This will encourage your rabbit to produce droppings as he munches, just like the wild rabbit. Most houserabbit owners find the litter tray is the best place to put hay. If you are using a cage, you could fix a hayrack over the tray, but, once you abandon the cage, you will find the tray to be the most convenient hay dispenser. Obviously, you will need to put fresh hay in the litter tray every day.

Grooming

Most of the time, normal- and Rex-coated rabbits take care of their own fur, but they will need assistance from you when they are

TOILETING TROUBLES

Julian and Caroline Turner, from Durham, tried their best to litter-train their Miniature Lop, Jenna, but just ended up confusing her…

"We adore Jenna, but when we first tried to train her to use a litter tray, we had dreadful problems. We started off with wood shavings in the tray. She used it, but she also loved digging, and we ended up with shavings all over the kitchen.

"Eventually, we hit on the idea of using kitchen paper instead. Jenna started off well, but we changed the paper and rinsed the tray every time she passed urine – to reduce the smell. She stopped using the tray altogether and started to mess all over the kitchen.

"It was only when we asked a local houserabbit expert for help that we realised it was us getting it all wrong, not Jenna. By cleaning the tray every time, we were totally confusing her. We had to clean the floor with a solution of biological washing powder to remove any smells that would encourage her to toilet on the floor again, and then put cat litter, topped with hay, in her tray.

"Within a couple of days, we had a litter-trained rabbit who was most relieved that she always knew where to find her loo!"

moulting. Moulting rabbits shed vast amounts of fur, and grooming will speed up the removal of dead, loose hair. Heavily moulting rabbits need grooming every day.

Brush your rabbit regularly, so that he becomes accustomed to it. For routine use, you can use a soft-bristled brush or one of the new, rubber brushes marketed for dogs and horses. These work really well on rabbits, even those who normally hate being groomed.

For moulting rabbits, try slicker brushes or cat moulting-combs, which have teeth of two lengths. These combs are very effective at removing the dead undercoat.

Pay particular attention to the area around the tail, where the fur is thickest and takes longest to moult out.

Long-haired rabbits are much harder work, and the best way to learn how to care for the coat is to get a demonstration from a rabbit rescue centre or an experienced breeder.

Adult, pedigree Cashmere Lops and Swiss Fox should have plenty of the long, guard hairs in their coats and these don't mat quite so easily. However, most long-haired rabbits kept as pets (and all young, long-haired breeds) have soft coats that mat easily and require frequent, thorough grooming.

- To groom a long-haired rabbit, start off with a wide-toothed comb and go over the whole animal.
- Then repeat with a finer-toothed comb.
- Finally, use a flea comb to groom the areas prone to matting – under the chin, inside the front legs, and around the vent area.
- It can take up to 20 to 40 minutes a day to groom a long-haired rabbit, so, if you would struggle to set this time aside, you may like to clip the coat completely every four to six weeks.

Grooming kit: a comb and a soft bristle brush or a rubber brush are used for routine grooming, but a slicker (middle, top) will be required during the moulting period.

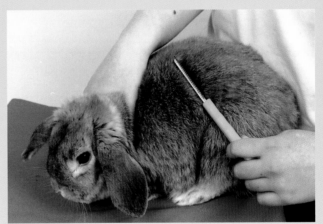

A normal-coated rabbit will need a quick but thorough brush and comb to remove dead hair.

Don't forget the belly! Cradling the rabbit securely will give you easy access to this area.

GROOMING A LONG-HAIRED RABBIT

1. The long-haired rabbit will need a thorough groom with a slicker to remove all tangles.

2. A small, fine-toothed comb should be used on the legs, under the chin, and around the vent.

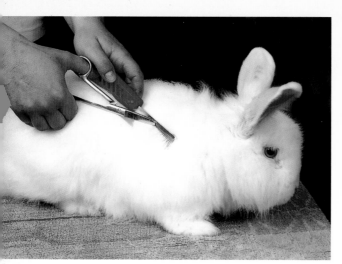

3. If clipping a pet, hold a comb underneath the scissors to protect the skin.

4. Finish off by combing through the coat.

Clipping

Some rescue centres or breeders will clip rabbits for a fee. You can do it yourself but it is best to be shown how, before you attempt it. Always use a comb to protect the skin, and carefully clip off the hair with scissors.

Round-tipped scissors are safer, but they don't penetrate mats as well. Normal dog clippers clog up when used on rabbits, although specially adapted blades are available.

EVERY MONTH

As well as daily observation of your rabbit, it is a good idea to perform a more extensive, home health check every month. A notebook is useful to write down anything you notice. You can combine this with routine grooming.

Look at and feel your rabbit all over, including his face and jaw. Get to know what his tummy feels like normally, and run your fingers over his legs and paws. Have any new lumps or bumps checked by the vet.

Comb through his fur looking for dandruff or loose, moulting fur. Check that the insides of the front paws are clean and dry – sometimes, the only clue to eye or nasal discharge is matting of the fur on the front paws.

Next inspect the claws. If the nails protrude beyond the fur line, they are too long and need clipping. Your veterinarian can teach you how to do this at home.

Have a quick look at your rabbit's hocks. It is normal to have a small patch of pink, callused skin underneath the fold of hair at the point of the hock, but broken or red skin is abnormal and should be investigated.

Rabbits of both sexes have a deep pouch on either side of the vent, which secretes a dark-coloured, smelly, waxy substance. This pouch should be gently cleaned with a damp cotton bud every couple of months.

If the rabbit's nails protrude beyond the fur line, they are too long.

Gently push the toes to expose the full nail, and clip a little off the end.

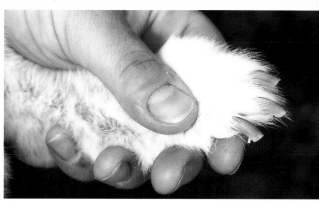

Short, neat nails.

The teeth should be even, with sharp edges.

Teeth

Check your rabbit's front teeth by gently drawing back his lips. The teeth should be even, with chisel-sharp edges, and any overgrowth will protrude over the other set of teeth. Overgrown upper incisors tend to grow back into the mouth, and you won't see them unless you look properly.

You will not be able to see the back teeth, but you can look for signs of problems, such as a constantly wet chin, lumps along the jaw, or the rabbit resenting your touching his head. Young rabbits, or those with a history of dental problems, should have their teeth checked more frequently.

Weight check

It is also worth weighing your rabbit regularly. Small bunnies can be weighed fairly accurately in the kitchen scales, but big rabbits are more difficult.

You can get an idea by weighing yourself on the bathroom scales and then weighing yourself holding the rabbit. Deduct the first weight from the second to find out how much your rabbit weighs. However, accurate weighing may require a trip to the veterinarian.

RABBIT SUPPLIES

Part of your care routine will include stocking up on supplies for your houserabbit.

Hay

Hay is an essential for your bunny. Good hay is sweet-smelling and dust-free. It can also be difficult to find, especially following a wet summer. Hay sold in pet shops is often of poor quality and stables are frequently a better place to buy from. Try ringing a local riding school, livery stable, or urban farm, and ask if you can buy some hay. Some rabbit rescue centres will sell hay to rabbit owners.

Any significant change in weight should be investigated by your vet.

A quarter of a bale will keep a single rabbit going for several weeks. Store the hay in a paper or hessian sack in a dry, cool area. A garage or dry shed is ideal.

Kiln-dried grass can be used as well as, or instead of, hay. You can purchase small bags of it from most pet shops, but, if you have several rabbits or lots of storage space, you might prefer to buy a large bale from an outlet selling horse food.

Cat litter
Deciding upon the most suitable cat litter for houserabbits is a remarkably controversial issue. In the UK, wood-based, pelleted cat litter is usually recommended. It is light and easy to handle, it absorbs odour well, it is easy to dispose of, and it can also be composted. It is easy to obtain and harmless if eaten by the rabbit.

There have been concerns that exposure to the aromatic hydrocarbons given off by pine products can be harmful to rabbits. This is a particularly controversial issue in the US. However, these worries are based upon research conducted on laboratory rats and mice. The results have little relevance to a houserabbit using a litter tray in a well-ventilated, domestic environment. Any biological effects are likely to be limited to a slight increase in liver enzyme activity, which is not necessarily harmful (it is comparable to a human enjoying a regular glass of wine). If you are particularly concerned, you may want to change to a different kind of litter or have your rabbit's liver function checked by a simple blood test.

Paper-based litters are often cited as an alternative to wood-based ones, but, in fact, they have a similar potential for producing aromatic hydrocarbons and many people report less satisfactory absorption and odour control than with pine-based products.

Corn-cob and hemp litters are also available, but cases of intestinal obstruction have been reported when rabbits have eaten them, so these should be avoided. Clumping cat litters, usually made of clay, pose a similar threat and are definitely best avoided.

Food
When purchasing rabbit food, check the use-by date and do not buy a bag that will not be eaten before this date is reached. Store rabbit food in a dry, cool, dark place, and, if you transfer the food into a plastic or metal container, remember to clean the container between each batch of food.

CHAPTER SIX

HEALTHY EATING

As a pet owner, you do not have to have an understanding of the mechanics of how rabbits digest food, but doing so will help put things into place. It is only really vital to remember one fact about the rabbit diet – rabbits are designed to eat grass!

THE DIGESTIVE SYSTEM

The rabbit digestive system is cunningly designed to extract the basic building blocks of protein, fat, carbohydrate, water, vitamins, and minerals from nutritionally low-value plant material. The system divides into two halves, the upper and lower digestive systems.

The upper digestive system consists of mouth, oesophagus, stomach and small intestine, while the lower digestive system, or hind gut, comprises the caecum and the colon.

Upper digestive system

The upper digestive system works just like ours. Food enters the mouth and passes down the oesophagus into the stomach, where the digestive process begins. The chewed-up food, mixed with gastric juices (ingesta), then moves into the small intestine. There are two points of interest in the upper digestive system. Firstly, rabbits cannot vomit, and secondly, rabbit teeth grow continuously. Grass is highly abrasive, so, if the teeth did not continue to grow, they would be worn away.

Lower digestive system

The lower digestive system deals with food in a special way. Semi-digested food enters the colon from the small intestine, where it is sorted into two parts. Indigestible, large fibre particles are of no further use to the rabbit, and they are directed straight on through the colon. After water has been extracted, this fibrous material emerges as the hard faecal droppings resembling raisins.

Liquid and non-fibrous particles, however, are diverted into the caecum. The caecum is, basically, an enormous fermentation chamber (rabbits are 'hind-gut fermentors'), and it is the powerhouse of the digestive system. Here, the ingesta is fermented by billions of friendly bacteria, releasing otherwise inaccessible nutrients from plant cells. Some of these nutrients are absorbed across the wall of the caecum; the rest are packaged up into the special droppings called caecotrophs, which are eaten by the rabbit as they emerge from the anus.

Caecotrophs

The caecotroph is a concentrated packet of nutritional goodness. Teeming with bacteria, the soft, smelly, dark caecotroph is covered in a layer of mucus. Once swallowed by the bunny, the caecotroph sits in the stomach for several hours. Eventually, the stomach acid erodes the mucus covering, releasing the nutrients within (mainly amino acids and vitamins), making them available for absorption. The stomach acid also kills most of the bacteria.

Although complex, this two-stage digestive process has several advantages. It enables rapid processing of vegetable material without the need for storing large amounts of fibre, which would be impossible in a small animal like the rabbit. Also, the coprophagic process of eating and digesting caecotrophs can take place in the safety and privacy of the burrow, away from predators. Finally, by utilising bacterial fermentation, rabbits enjoy a diet far richer in protein than would otherwise be possible from grass and other vegetation.

Caecotrophs (left) are darker and more shiny than the normal, round, faecal droppings (right).

Daily grazing on lush, fresh grass is not always possible for houserabbits.

YOUR RABBIT'S DIET

Feeding your rabbit need not be complicated. The ideal diet is based on what grass provides:

- High fibre (at least 20 per cent) to sustain normal gut movement
- Moderate protein (12 to 15 per cent) for body repair and growth
- Low levels of fat, starch and sugar
- Abrasive action on teeth.

Grass should make up the bulk of your rabbit's diet. Fresh grass is wonderful, but, unless your rabbit has daily access to a lawn-run, you will have to pick a large pile of grass every day.

Dried grass, either as hay or kiln-dried grass, is a perfectly acceptable alternative and far more practical for most houserabbit owners. It doesn't matter too much what form the grass is in, just make sure your bunny eats lots of it and always has access to as much as he wants.

already feeding a commercially prepared pellet or mix that contains alfalfa.

Kiln-dried grass

Kiln-dried grass is made by drying fresh grass much more rapidly than the traditional hay-making process. The final product is green in colour, with a higher nutritional value than meadow or seed hay, but it is less rich than alfalfa hay. Popular with horse owners for several years, this form of hay is rapidly gaining favour with rabbit owners and it is now available in small packs as well as horse-size bales.

Commercial foods

For convenience, you may feed limited quantities of commercially prepared rabbit foods in addition to the grass/hay base. Alternatively, you may want to provide a natural diet, offering a selection of fresh, dark, leafy greens and vegetables every day. A healthy rabbit, eating a healthy varied diet, does not need any vitamin or mineral supplementation.

Commercially prepared rabbit foods are available in several different forms. The traditional choice is a rabbit mix, a muesli-like mixture of different ingredients. These mixes can make a useful contribution to a balanced diet as long as the rabbit eats all the components.

Unfortunately, many bunnies are 'selective feeders', picking out the ingredients they like and rejecting the rest. Selective feeding can lead to an unbalanced diet, which puts the rabbit at risk of calcium deficiency if he rejects the vitamin-D-fortified components.

If you feed a mix, you must ensure that your rabbit eats it all, and always choose a reputable brand that has been expertly formulated. If your rabbit will not eat it all, or if you have two rabbits living together and each picks out

Hay is a convenient way of feeding grass to indoor bunnies.

Hay

There are several types of hay. Meadow hay is cut from permanent pastureland. It is soft in texture and contains a variety of natural herbs and weeds. Seed hay is grown as a crop, and so it consists of just one type of grass. In the UK, this is usually rye grass; in the US, timothy grass. It tends to be longer and harder in texture than meadow hay.

Alfalfa hay is rarely used in the UK, but it is more popular in the US. It is much richer than meadow or seed hay, and can be fattening. Do not use it if your rabbit is overweight, has had problems with excess calcium, or if you are different ingredients, you should consider switching to a pelleted or extruded product.

Rabbit pellets and extruded foods solve the problem of selective feeding because each nugget is identical in composition. Until recently, the main problem with both these options was that rabbit owners felt that they looked 'too boring'. In fact, most rabbits find them highly palatable, particularly extruded foods that are rapidly increasing in popularity. However, you may notice an increase in water consumption if your rabbit eats mainly extruded food.

FOOD LABELS

Animal foods must be labelled as either 'complementary' or 'complete'. Complete foods should meet all the nutritional requirements of the animal, whereas complementary products are designed to be fed in conjunction with other foodstuffs. Most rabbit foods are complementary, designed to be fed with hay or greens.

Be wary of rabbit foods labelled as complete. While some are high-quality products meeting all the nutritional requirements of rabbits, others are mediocre mixtures with inadequate protein and fibre content. Even if you feed a nutritionally complete food, there are other reasons why your rabbit should have constant access to hay; the molar teeth need the grinding action of chewing grass-like material, and foraging for hay keeps the bunny busy. Therefore, feeding any commercial rabbit food in isolation is not recommended unless your rabbit cannot, or will not, eat hay or grass.

COMPLEMENTARY DRIED FOODS

Commercial pellets: a good choice for selective feeders.

Dried grass: a practical alternative to fresh grass.

Commercial mix: a balanced diet, provided the rabbit eats all the ingredients and does not pick out his favourite bits!

Extruded: another option for selective bunnies, this highly palatable food is growing in popularity.

THE 'HAY-AND-VEGGIE' DIET

This diet consists of ad-lib hay and a heap of leafy greens and vegetables every day, with only very small quantities of commercial food. It is a very good way of feeding pet rabbits and it is popular with houserabbit enthusiasts, especially in the US. This diet suits many older rabbits, for whom conventional rabbit food seems to be too rich. It is particularly suitable for rabbits who produce excess caecotrophs, leading to 'sticky bottom syndrome'.

Unless your rabbit has been reared on green food since weaning, you will have to introduce green food very gradually. Allow several weeks for the process to be completed and follow the following basic rules.

• Introduce vegetables one at a time, in small quantities at first
• Grass is perfect, but it needs to be a decent length – not lawn clippings
• Don't pick greens from polluted verges or anywhere where dogs foul.

Choose from this list of foods and feed a selection every day, including at least one or two dark leafy vegetables.

Green food should be introduced gradually to your rabbit's diet.

Greens
• Clover
• Celery
• Coriander
• Dandelion greens and flowers
• Docks
• Escarole
• Green peppers
• Ground elder
• Groundsel
• Mint
• Parsley
• Pea pods
• Plantain
• Radish tops
• Raspberry leaves
• Romaine lettuce (not iceberg or light-coloured leaf)
• Spinach and kale may be given in small quantities
• Spring greens
• Sow thistle
• Sweetcorn
• Watercress.

Fruits
Feed one daily, fresh or dried. You should aim for one tablespoonful per 2 kg (4 lbs) of your rabbit's bodyweight.
• Apple
• Banana
• Melon
• Peach
• Pear
• Pineapple
• Strawberries.

The hay-and-veggie diet in action in a multi-rabbit household. Each plate feeds two to three bunnies per meal.

QUANTITY

Indoor bunnies require less energy from their food than wild rabbits. Our neutered houserabbits don't have to keep themselves warm, breed, fight, or forage for food over several acres! Add to this the tendency of houserabbits to beg, and it is little wonder that our rabbits are getting fatter! Obesity is extremely common in pet rabbits and it carries serious health risks – decreased life expectancy, higher-risk patients for surgery, higher risk of flystrike, and premature arthritis.

Avoid obesity by feeding the correct amount of food for the rabbit's size and activity. All rabbits should eat as much hay or grass as they wish. If you are using a commercial food, there will be instructions on the packet, but, as a rough guide, a 1 kg (2 lb) dwarf may need only an eggcupful per day, and a medium-sized, 3 kg (6 lb) rabbit about a third to a half of a standard 5-inch (12.5-cm) rabbit bowl. For vegetables and greens, build a pile to match the size of the rabbit each day. You can mix and match – there's nothing wrong with going half way towards the hay-and-veggie diet! Every rabbit is different, and you will have to adjust the amount of food you give according to your rabbit's weight. It is not always easy to determine this yourself, and it is worth discussing with your vet what is an ideal weight for your own bunny. A weight-reduction diet may be necessary. Ideally, the bunny should be well muscled, but you should be able to feel his ribs and backbone if you stroke him firmly. He should produce plenty of even-sized droppings; with only very occasional caecotrophs left uneaten. Pads of fat around the top of the legs or at the back of the neck, or an enormous dewlap, can indicate obesity. Internal fat is more difficult to assess, but a large pot-belly may indicate a problem. Rabbits with round heads often have chunky bodies, but no bunny should have a tiny head on a large body. If your bunny looks wider than he is long, he is seriously fat.

A little fruit is a welcome addition to a fresh-veg diet.

If you cannot feel your rabbit's ribs and backbone when you stroke him, then a diet is needed!

HEALTHY TREATS

Rabbits love sugary foods, and some acquire tastes for the most bizarre foodstuffs – there are rabbits who like beer and curry! Amusing this may be, but it is a bad idea to start feeding human foods to your rabbit. Too much starch or sugar can wreak havoc with the sensitive bacterial population in the gut, and, like us, rabbits can suffer from tooth decay as well as putting on excess weight.

Stick to healthy treats, such as chunks of carrot or broccoli, perhaps a nibble of Ryvita, apple cores, carrot/swede/turnip peelings, and cauliflower stalks. These healthy treats can be fed frequently once your bunny is used to them. The various treats marketed for rabbits, ranging from milk-based yoghurt drops to sticks of cereals and grains, should be used in strict moderation, or avoided entirely.

Of course, your rabbit will have other ideas and it's so hard to resist an appealing, begging bunny. But it is really, really important to be strict. If you must give in, limit extras to a maximum daily treat of one pea-sized piece of cake or cookie, a one-inch (2.5-cm) chunk of banana, or a couple of unsalted peanuts. No more; anything extra risks both his waistline and his health.

THE HEALTHY GUT

The successful functioning of the digestive system relies on a healthy population (flora) of beneficial bacteria in the hind gut. If the delicate bacterial population becomes unbalanced, and 'bad bugs' multiply out of control, serious or even fatal diarrhoea can develop within hours.

This can occur if the rabbit is stressed or otherwise unwell, after treatment with some antibiotics, or especially after changes in diet. Gut bacteria need time to adapt to different foods, so you should never change your rabbit's diet suddenly.

When introducing new foods, do it slowly. Offer only a very small portion of the new food at first, mixing it well with the usual diet. To switch between different brands of mix/pellets, gradually increase the ratio of new food to old over at least one week, preferably two. Constant access to hay will cushion dietary changes.

Prebiotics and probiotics

To help keep the gut healthy, some feed manufacturers add a food supplement that will support beneficial gut bacteria. These are called prebiotics. Also available are probiotics, which actually contain friendly bacteria. Probiotics are designed to be fed to bunnies whose gut flora is

A carrot is a healthy treat that won't cause your bunny to pile on the pounds.

SPECIAL NEEDS

Excess caecotrophs

This is commonly called 'sticky bottom syndrome', because you will find a lot of excess caecotrophs either on the floor or caked to the rabbit's bottom. It is very common in overfed rabbits. Increasing the proportion of hay in the diet, and gradually replacing commercial foods with vegetables and greens, usually solves the problem, but a change of food brand may be needed.

Other causes of excess caecotrophs are obesity, reduced mobility, and dental disease. However, dietary problems are by far the most common cause and it is worth trying a change in diet. If this doesn't work, seek veterinary advice.

It's really important to recognise that excess caecotrophs are not diarrhoea, which is much more liquid in consistency. Older books may tell you to withdraw green food if soft droppings occur, whereas the correct treatment for excess caecotrophs is completely the opposite.

Any dietary change should be gradual, to avoid stomach upsets.

in jeopardy, for example during illness or antibiotic therapy. However, it is difficult to ensure these probiotics will survive transit through the highly acidic stomach.

Traditionally, live yoghurt has been used as a probiotic agent. However, it is inadvisable to feed any dairy produce to rabbits. The latest commercial probiotics are much more sophisticated, containing a more logical species of bacteria in a form that is claimed to resist stomach acid. Although distasteful to us, the best probiotic for a poorly bunny is probably caecotrophs from a healthy rabbit, although there are, of course, concerns about transmitting disease from the 'donor' rabbit to the recipient.

A diet that is high in hay and fresh vegetables should reduce instances of excessive caecotrophs.

Young rabbits

Rabbits less than 12 weeks of age need careful feeding. They are growing rapidly, but their digestive systems are very sensitive.

Several factors make baby rabbits vulnerable to digestive upsets. At weaning, the gut bacteria have to switch from dealing with milk to vegetation. To make matters worse, during this period, young rabbits do not have the highly acidic environment in their stomachs to protect them from gut infections. Finally, baby rabbits are exposed to stressful experiences, such as changes of home and separation from littermates. Fatal tummy upsets are common in young rabbits purchased from pet shops, who have to cope with the double dose of stress and dietary change. Hence, any changes to the diet must be made even more cautiously than with adult rabbits.

Even if you intend to switch to the hay-and-veggie diet later on, young rabbits will need commercial rabbit food to support their high growth rate. Rapidly growing rabbits can be fed as much as they will eat, but don't allow them to start being picky or reject any part of the mix.

You may choose one of the specially formulated 'junior' foods, but any good-quality rabbit food should be adequate. There is no need to avoid giving green food to baby rabbits, as long as it is introduced slowly and carefully. Youngsters – like all rabbits – should have free access to hay.

Overweight rabbits

Seriously overweight rabbits should be slimmed under veterinary supervision. Typically, you will be advised to cut out pellets/mix completely, and feed hay and water alone for a few weeks. However, some experts feel that rabbits should not lose weight quite so rapidly and that the maximum rate of weight loss should be one to

Youngsters, such as this 16-week-old, need commercial food to support their rapid growth.

Supervised play sessions in the garden will help to keep your rabbit fit and lean.

two per cent loss per week. This may be ideal in mild to moderate cases of obesity, but seriously fat rabbits do need to shift weight quickly, at least until they can take care of their personal hygiene requirements. After that, you can take things more steadily.

If your rabbit is just a bit podgy rather than obese, you can simply halve his ration of mix/pellets. He should have unlimited hay as usual and you could use this opportunity to gradually increase his intake of green food, to mimic the natural diet of the rabbit. Fattening treats, such as peanuts and sunflower seeds, have to go!

Encourage your rabbit to exercise – fat rabbits are often lazy, which makes the whole situation worse. Make him run up the stairs, play games with him, and take him in the garden for a supervised run.

Calcium balance problems

On a balanced, healthy diet, most rabbits take care of their own calcium balance. Too much calcium can be as harmful as too little, so, if your rabbit is diagnosed with calcium-related problems, you will need to work closely with your vet to design a strategy to tackle the problem. It is likely to involve dietary adjustment.

For example, a calcium-deficient rabbit may be encouraged to eat foods rich in calcium, be prevented from selective feeding of rabbit mix by switching to a pelleted or extruded food, be encouraged to sunbathe outside every day, and be given a vitamin supplement. A rabbit suffering from excess calcium must be taken off any vitamin supplements, may be taken off all commercially prepared foods, and restricted to grass, hay and vegetables low in calcium.

CHAPTER SEVEN

RABBIT BEHAVIOUR

One of the greatest pleasures about living with a houserabbit is the opportunity to watch these animals at close quarters. Rabbits communicate mainly by body language, and your rabbit may be trying to tell you something by what he does, as well as by emitting audible sounds.

THE RUNNING RABBIT

Your rabbit runs in several different ways. If you accidentally startle him, he may dash back to his cage or behind the furniture in a blind panic. If he's exploring a new area of the house, he will go very cautiously, his ears pointing forward. After all, he doesn't know there's not a fox behind the door! Young rabbits sometimes revert to their baby crawl when they are uncertain, which is most endearing.

Once your rabbit is confident, he will bob about with a standard cheeky hop. If he's feeling full of the joys of life, he may race around the room for sheer pleasure, sometimes with a kick and twist referred to as 'binkying'.

At other times, this joyful gallop will start from a standing leap off all fours, with the rabbit twisting round to land in the opposite direction. Some rabbits will binky back at you if you leap up and down in front of them, but make sure nobody can see you do this or they are liable to think you have completely lost your marbles!

THE RELAXED RABBIT

A relaxed rabbit isn't difficult to spot. You'll find him lying on his side or tummy, with his hind legs kicked out behind him.

This basic position varies from a watchful 'I'm relaxed, but watching you' pose, with ears straight up, swivelling towards the source of any sound, to the 'almost asleep' position, with chin resting on the floor and eyes half closed. If he's feeling really chilled out, he might flake completely, lying flat on his side with his head on the floor. Some rabbits literally fling themselves down dramatically into this 'playing dead' position – you may think for a moment that your rabbit has expired.

THE ALERT RABBIT

At the other end of the scale is the bunny on alert – sitting or standing in a lookout position, nose twitching, ears directed towards any source

The relaxed rabbit will lie down with his legs kicked out behind him.

The 'play dead' pose of a really chilled-out bunny gives many novice owners quite a shock!

of sound. This is a rabbit using his entire armoury of sensory equipment to look for danger. If he's worried, he may thump the ground hard with his hind feet. This is the alarm signal of the wild rabbit, which tells his warren-mates to get down the burrow immediately. The noise is amazingly loud inside the home.

A really terrified rabbit may crouch down, eyes bulging, ears right back. Wild rabbits do this if they get stuck in the middle of a field in the vicinity of a predator – pretending to be invisible may be safer than attempting the sprint to the burrow.

TAIL TALK

Tail position is often a giveaway about what your rabbit is thinking. If your rabbit holds out his tail behind himself, with his ears flat to his head, he's angry. This is often seen when you introduce a new rabbit too quickly; it is the prelude to a fight. You may also see it if you intrude into your rabbit's territory – don't expect to be made welcome! If you provoke a rabbit displaying this pattern of behaviour, he may well launch himself at you and 'box' you with his front feet, and if he's really irate, he'll use his teeth as well!

A tail held well up over the back indicates courting behaviour. Female rabbits often flirt around males with their tail bolt upright when they are receptive to mating. You may see this behaviour before your rabbit is neutered. Beware the un-neutered male rabbit circling your feet, grunting or honking, with his tail in the air. You are very likely to get sprayed with urine at any moment.

Comically, houserabbits sometimes give a cheeky flick to the tail when they have been told off, or are interrupted before doing something they shouldn't!

The alert rabbit in the lookout position – ready to respond to any danger.

ATTENTION SEEKING

Many rabbits will demand attention by 'presenting' to their owner. The bunny will approach you, and, as he reaches your hand or feet, he will put his chin down, with his ears flat on his head.

Your likely response will be to rub his nose, which is exactly what he intended. This behaviour often indicates a dominant rabbit – and it also demonstrates how smart your rabbit is, getting just what he wants from you.

The initial greeting between rabbits who already know one another is a gentle 'nose nudge'. You often find rabbits do this to their owners as well, especially if you have been out all day or away for longer.

A harder nudge indicates that you are sitting in your rabbit's way and he's asking you to move. If you stay put, he is likely to nip you as he would another rabbit who is blocking his path.

GROOMING

Many rabbits like to lick and groom their owners. This is a gesture of friendship and acceptance – rabbits who like each other lie together and groom one another.

Unfortunately, normal rabbit grooming uses the teeth as well as the tongue, so don't be surprised if a rabbit nibbles you or your clothing in between licking you. You can see this nibbling action if you watch your rabbit cleaning himself – he will lean over and use it to clean the fur on his rump.

It is fascinating to watch a rabbit groom himself. Grooming is a fastidious ritual. Starting with a little flick of the front paws, the rabbit will sit on his hind legs and proceed to wash his face with his paws, making sure his ears are well cleaned by pulling them forwards with his paws so he can reach the tips. He will then groom round the back of his neck, scratching with his hind foot and nibbling and licking the fur on his neck.

Your rabbit will clean the insides of his ears by digging into them with his hind foot and then licking his paws clean. He will carefully wash his front paws by licking, and then his hind feet are brought forward in turn, toes spread to get right between them.

Bunny buddies often greet each other with nose nudges.

VOCAL SOUNDS

It is easy to forget that rabbits have a vocal language. Rabbit vocalizations are much quieter than human language, but, over time, you will hear your rabbit making all sorts of strange and wonderful noises.

Some sounds are self-explanatory – an angry rabbit may growl at you, or an un-neutered buck may honk or hum while circling your feet.

However, there are other, more subtle noises. For example, your bunny may give little squeaks when in the process of twisting round to groom or take caecotrophs.

There are two types of sound connected with teeth grinding, and their meaning could not be more different. A rapid, gentle grinding indicates that your bunny is content – you might hear (or feel) this noise if you are rubbing your rabbit's cheeks when he has asked you for a head-rub. However, slower, harder teeth grinding is a sign of a rabbit in pain, and it is usually associated with a rabbit that is clearly unwell, sitting hunched up or acting in a withdrawn manner.

Hopefully, you will never hear your rabbit scream. This is a remarkably loud, almost primeval shriek. It is nearly always an expression of sheer terror from a rabbit in fear of his life, but, just occasionally, one finds a rabbit that has learnt that letting out a squeal gets the attention of his owner better than anything else. Who said rabbits were daft?

RABBIT ENTERTAINMENT

It is vital that your houserabbit is able to express his full repertoire of natural behaviour, otherwise he will become bored and he will inevitably take out his frustration on your home. Part of the fun of owning a houserabbit is devising new amusements for him! Remember, a busy rabbit is a happy rabbit...

An activity ball will satisfy your rabbit's natural foraging instinct.

Foraging

In the wild, a rabbit will spend several hours a day foraging for food. Encourage your rabbit to spend as much time and energy as possible obtaining his food. Rather than presenting his food in a bowl, try these popular ways of making your rabbit 'forage' for his meals.

- A 'buster cube' is a hollow plastic ball or cube with several small holes. You push food into the holes and the bunny has to push the cube around the floor to make the food fall out, one piece at a time. Most rabbits quickly become experts, although a few can't – or won't – get the hang of it.

Stuffing hay into a jar will make your bunny work harder for his food.

- Hide the food ration among the hay, either in the litter tray or in a large cardboard box or basket.
- Stuff hay into a jar or can, or through a metal napkin ring or similar, so that your rabbit has to work hard to get to the strands of hay.

Chewing

There is no doubt that it can take many months of training before your rabbit learns to turn his teeth on to the things you want him to, rather than things you don't. All rabbits chew, but some make particularly enthusiastic shredding machines.

Increasing the foraging time, and encouraging your rabbit to chomp through large amounts of hay every day, will help keep his teeth productively occupied. However, you will still have to provide your houserabbit with plenty of items to gnaw on – such as untreated wood, cardboard, old newspapers and magazines, all of which are safe and suitable. Old telephone directories are particular favourites. With persistence, inappropriate chewing should stop.

Digging

The burrowing, digging instinct is strong in all rabbits. They love exploring dark nooks and crannies. Supply some substitutes, such as rolled-up carpet offcuts, or the large-bore, plastic sewage piping already mentioned.

Make a 'dig box' by cutting a peep hole at least half way up the end of a large, sturdy cardboard box. Put some wood shavings, or even dried peat, inside the box to the depth of a couple of inches (a few centimetres) and loosely fill the box with hay or straw. Your rabbit will enter the box, turn around to face the peep hole, and have a lovely time digging and playing.

If he goes at it with real gusto, fit the floor of the box with a piece of plywood or hardboard, to stop him digging through the cardboard and depositing the contents of the box on the carpet!

A large, deep wicker laundry basket filled with hay can perform a similar function, with the added attraction that the basket itself can be edible – choose one made of untreated straw, not the stained type. Both will keep most rabbits amused for hours.

If you provide your rabbit with something safe to chew, you may prevent him from destroying other, unsuitable items in the house.

Jumping on and off furniture makes a good rabbit work-out!

Children's rattle toys are a favourite with many houserabbits.

Jumping

Exercise is vitally important for your rabbit's physical and mental well being. Permanently caged rabbits suffer from weak bones and spines. Rabbits must have the opportunity to run and jump. Most houserabbits get plenty of exercise, creating an improvised jumping course from household furniture. However, some obese, older rabbits are distinctly lazy, and you may have to bribe your bunny to run up and down the stairs, or to hop over small obstacles to get sufficient exercise.

Throw toys

Quite what wild rabbits toss and throw we are not sure, but pet rabbits seem to enjoy throwing baby rattles, cat bells, and toilet-roll inner tubes, particularly if they are thrown or rolled towards them, when they may be tossed back with a definite grunt.

CHAPTER EIGHT

TRAINING & TROUBLESHOOTING

Rabbits are remarkably intelligent and they are perfectly capable of being trained. However, they are also bright enough to do things in their own way. Consequently, you will have to harness the rabbit's natural behaviour patterns, using positive reinforcement as well as persuasion to train your housebunny successfully.

Achieving the goal of a mature, well-behaved bunny, enjoying the free run of at least one or two rooms without constant supervision, will not be achieved overnight. Just like bringing up children, there will be times when you are frustrated and things are not going well – this is all part of being a houserabbit owner.

However, do not despair. Nearly all problems can be sorted out with patience and persistence, and, given time, you can live in harmony with your bunny, looking back on his naughty, youthful antics through rose-tinted spectacles.

THE GOLDEN RULES
There are four golden rules:
- All training should be reward-based. Reward desired behaviour immediately, with verbal praise, a gentle stroke, or a tasty treat.

Make permitted chew items so attractive that they are more interesting to play with than chewing the furniture.
- Never hit your rabbit, never grab hold of him, and never shout at him close up. This will only ruin your relationship. Even a tap on the nose could provoke an aggressive reaction from an assertive rabbit. Instead, interrupt undesirable behaviour with the

Anything left on the floor is fair game – if it gets chewed, it's your fault!

Rabbits are not born with the knowledge of how to behave in a human home – youngsters must be taught what is acceptable conduct.

you will need to reinforce the command with a quick squirt from a water pistol. Alternatively, physically remove your rabbit from the area.

This is one reason why it is essential, in the early days, to give your rabbit your undivided attention. While he is learning this command you must be able to reinforce it. Your bunny will soon learn that "No!" means, "Stop what you are doing right now!" Unfortunately, rabbits are clever enough to realise that, when their owner is cooking or on the telephone etc., they can get away with all sorts of behaviour without being interrupted. Hopefully, once he has reliably learnt the "No!" command, he will always respond, not realising there are times when you can't back up your verbal command.

"No!" command (see below).

• Be consistent. If you laugh when your rabbit shreds the telephone directory, how is he supposed to know that he isn't meant to chew the library book on the coffee table? If you don't want something chewed, keep it out of reach. Anything left on the floor is fair game.

• Be patient. Your bunny is unlikely to turn into a paragon of lapine virtue until he is fully grown. He'll be physically mature at six months, but won't behave like an adult until he is 12 to 18 months at least.

"NO!"

The "No!" command is used to stop your rabbit pursuing any unwanted action. Any sudden loud noise, such as clapping your hands or stamping your foot, followed by a firm "No!" should stop him in his tracks. As soon as he stops, reward his good behaviour and immediately offer him a more attractive alternative. If he doesn't stop,

Rabbits might look like adorable little angels, but training – and vigilance – are always required.

BORN TO BE WILD

Jaffa, an eight-year-old, neutered Sussex Gold, lives with Linda Dykes in Liverpool. Although he is a beautifully behaved bunny now, his younger days were wild, to say the least!

Jaffa's youth was spent on one long mission of destruction!

"Jaffa's getting on in years now, and, although he can still be mischievous, he's a model houserabbit, who has convinced lots of people that an indoor rabbit is the pet they want. However, he's not always been as angelic. When he was younger, he was an absolute terror, who frequently went on the rampage!

"I adopted Jaffa when he was six months old and I was still a student. He lived with me in my student digs, with a puppy cage to go in when I was out. I made the classic mistake of letting him out whenever I was in the house, regardless of whether I had other things to do. Being a bright and determined bunny, he soon discovered that he could run riot if I was otherwise distracted. I shudder to think of the number of library books that were returned with nibbled covers, and the state of the valance on my bed (I know I like broderie anglaise, but that was ridiculous). Then there was the occasion, just after his first birthday, when he sneaked into my housemate's room and beheaded a rose given to her on Valentine's Day by her boyfriend. He also chewed her trainers and ate a half-finished essay. There were threats of rabbit pie that day, but it's difficult to stay angry with a bunny who then leaps on to your lap and starts to lick your chin.

"The vast majority of his misdemeanors were my fault – I simply wasn't supervising him closely enough. However, it was the telephone that provided Jaffa with his best opportunities for mass destruction. It didn't take him long to figure out that, when mum was tied to the wall talking to an unseen person, he could do whatever he liked. His favourite trick was to get into the wardrobe and chew the laces off shoes, although making holes in jeans came a close second.

"I couldn't use a water pistol in rented accommodation, so I kept a supply of rolled-up socks near the telephone and I would throw one at him if he ignored me when I was on the telephone!

"By the time he was 18 months old, Jaffa was far less destructive and could be left for reasonable periods unattended. By the time I bought my own house, he was two years old and we had dispensed with the cage. He now lives in the kitchen with his companion, Smuts, when I'm at work, but other than that, he's allowed the run of the house. That is, apart from my bedroom, which isn't bunny-proofed...

"Only last week he got into my bedroom and chomped through the telephone cable – I suppose it happens to us all from time to time!"

Jaffa with his good companion, Smuts.

If your rabbit realises that he can sometimes ignore the "No!" command, or if he is particularly determined, try a different strategy to deter him from his activities. See if the chew-repellent sprays sold for puppies and kittens will work, or try other strong-smelling, harmless substances, such as eucalyptus oil. However, persistence with command training, reinforced with a water pistol if necessary, is usually the best solution. Even the most determined bunnies will give up when they equate sofa nibbling with a dousing!

TROUBLESHOOTING

When you see typically endearing houserabbit behaviour, such as lounging in front of the fire, watching television from the sofa, or begging for treats, it is very easy to forget how much hard work is needed to complete the rabbit's training. All pet owners encounter behavioural problems from time to time, and their inability to cope with them is very high on the list of reasons why pet cats and dogs, as well as rabbits, are handed over to rescue organisations for rehoming.

Overcoming these difficulties may be far more simple than you think, and your role as a responsible pet owner is to try to work out the problems. However frustrated and upset you are, start by looking at the situation objectively.

• Is this normal behaviour?
• Is this acceptable behaviour?
• Are you doing something
  to cause or exacerbate the problem?

There may be a good reason for your rabbit's behaviour. Some of the most common problems are described below.

ADOLESCENCE

Rabbits reach puberty anywhere from three to six months of age. You will notice some marked changes in your bunny's behaviour and most of them will be undesirable. Living with a rabbit who is, effectively, going through a stage of life equating to that of a human teenager, has been aptly described as living with a "bunny from hell".

Males

Male rabbits will start to display territorial, courtship behaviour. Often, litter-training is abandoned and they start to scatter droppings all over the house. They may also 'chin' objects, to mark out their territory. Male rabbits mark out their chosen mate by spraying her with urine. In the absence of another rabbit, you may become the focus of your bunny's amorous advances.

Adolescence can be a testing time for owners. Pictured: six-month buck.

CALM AFTER THE STORM

An angelic baby bunny, Jasper Amos turned into an adolescent nightmare within months. In desperation, owners Megan and Justin Amos from Banbury, Oxon, even considered rehoming him, but, luckily, they discovered the key to his behaviour just in time…

"Jasper came to us when he was six weeks old. He was fabulous – friendly, extrovert, funny. He was so good with his litter-training we let him have the run of the living room within a few days. Everything was wonderful for about three months and all of our friends wanted to adopt him!

"Then it all began to unravel. It started with a few droppings scattered on the living room carpet. Then he began to urinate on the doormat. About the same time, he started to circle our feet and grunt madly. That was quite funny, until he tried to mate with my boyfriend's feet and bit his leg! After that, we couldn't walk around the house in bare feet and I didn't know what had happened to make him behave like this. We put up with it for a few more weeks, but then he started to spray. There were urine marks down the walls, on our clothes, and on the furniture. He had to stay in his cage the whole time and was miserable at being locked up.

"We were so desperate we telephoned a rabbit rescue centre and asked if they could take Jasper.

We were gutted, but felt it wasn't fair to keep him if he had to be caged. We live in a flat, so we couldn't even build him a run in the garden. We were so pleased when the lady at the rescue centre explained that all we needed to do was have Jasper castrated. We booked him in for his operation a few days later.

"Of course, things didn't go back to normal straight away. It took a few weeks for Jasper to stop spraying and trying to mate our feet. We had to work very hard to persuade him to confine his droppings to his litter tray, and that took several months. We were instructed to impress upon Jasper that his cage was his territory, so we didn't go anywhere near it when he was in residence.

"Fortunately, it worked – he didn't feel the need to leave droppings all over the place because he had his own secure space. Over the next few months, Jasper matured into a fabulous companion. He chewed the kitchen table, but otherwise was quite well behaved. He used to watch television with us and slept under our bed. When he died last year, we were devastated. He was only four, but he had severe dental problems. He was part of the family and our home feels empty without him. We're getting a new rabbit soon, but this time we're adopting a rescue bunny that has already been neutered."

Circling and humming around you is often a prelude to spraying and an attempt to mate with your feet. Beware, if your rabbit does not get his own way, he may bite, hard! He may also try mating with cuddly toys or footballs – in fact, anything he can mount is fair game.

Boy bunny behaviour can become very embarrassing, and, unsurprisingly, owners have been known to sneak past their rabbit in an effort to avoid an unwanted shower of extremely pungent rabbit urine.

Females

Female rabbits also display undesirable behaviour at puberty. Usually, they become territorial and aggressive. Typically, they will leap forward, growling loudly, to scratch and even bite if anyone ventures into their cage.

Also common are phantom pregnancies. Usually, your female rabbit will be very unapproachable at these times. She may be seen busily running around or digging, with a mouth full of hay, fur or other nest-building material.

Neutering has a calming effect on hormone-driven behaviour, and produces a more relaxed, companionable bunny.

Neutering

In both sexes, adolescent behaviour can sometimes be so severe that owners do not know how to cope. Sadly, some rabbits are even destroyed. However, as these behaviours are all driven by sex hormones, they should dramatically improve or even disappear altogether if the rabbit (male or female) is neutered. It is advisable to routinely neuter all houserabbits. Neutered rabbits are easier to house-train, less destructive, and less smelly – older males in particular have a rather pungent odour if they are not castrated.

Neutering won't change the underlying personality of an adult rabbit, nor maintain the babyish behaviour of a young rabbit. However, your neutered rabbit will be more willing to interact with you and he will be free from the frustration of the constant desire to find a mate. As well as the positive impact on behaviour, there are important health benefits of neutering, which are fully discussed in Chapter Eleven.

DESTRUCTIVE BEHAVIOUR

Chewing

As we have already seen, rabbits have a natural instinct to chew and to dig. If you cannot provide sufficient attractive outlets for this behaviour, it is inevitable that your rabbit will amuse himself with your furnishings instead. If you are supervising and training your rabbit correctly, he should have little opportunity to cause too much damage, and, if he does, you have probably given him too much freedom, too soon. Some rabbits take longer than others to learn acceptable habits. If your rabbit is intent on eating the contents of the living room, and you don't have time to watch his every move, try making the kitchen or bathroom his free-running area – in most homes, these areas are already relatively bunny-proof.

Chewing is a natural behaviour, so keep valued items out of reach.

Early handling can help to accustom your rabbit to being held – an action that he will naturally perceive as a threat.

Struggling

Very few rabbits enjoy being picked up. This is not really surprising – the only thing that picks up a wild rabbit is a fox or another predator. There are exceptions to every rule, and you will occasionally come across rabbits who love to snuggle with their owners. If you buy an eight-week-old baby rabbit and handle it every day, it may still grow up to hate being handled.

However, you can reduce the likelihood of this problem if you obtain a baby bunny from a breeder or rescue centre that regularly handles babies between the ages of 10 days and 6 weeks – which is thought to be the main socialisation period in rabbits.

Although struggling is an understandable response, the rabbit needs to learn how to tolerate routine handling. Ensure you pick him up confidently and correctly.

Have a supply of edible treats to hand. Pick up your bunny and immediately put him down again and give him a treat. Then pick him up again for a few seconds longer, and, as soon as he has relaxed, put him down and treat him again. Don't put him down if he is actually struggling – you are trying to teach him that he is rewarded for calm behaviour, not that he will be put down the moment he starts to struggle.

Biting

Rabbits have very sharp teeth and can inflict a painful bite. If your rabbit attacks you quite regularly, you need to ask yourself why. Some 'biting' is just your rabbit communicating in the way he would with another rabbit. If his

Never physically remove a territorial rabbit from his 'warren'. If you need to clean his cage, coax him out with a treat first.

nipping is a bit too hard, try letting out a squeal – just like his littermates would – and hope that he learns to nip a little less ferociously. Biting could also be caused by territorial aggression. We try constantly to reinforce the idea that our rabbit's cage is *his* territory. This can help with litter-training. However, it may also mean that the bunny will defend his territory aggressively.

Respect his space! Coax him out of the cage before you clean it and don't disturb him when he is in residence. Territorial aggression can be reduced, but not eliminated, by neutering.

Rabbits may bite when afraid. If a rabbit feels threatened and he is unable to flee, he might freeze or fight. Humans – especially children – who fail to recognise that a rabbit is frightened will often try to pick up a rabbit who has 'frozen'. Next time, the bunny has learnt that 'freezing' didn't work and he will attack instead.

If none of these situations seems to apply to your rabbit, and you are still being attacked, then it is probably a good idea to seek expert advice. Always have the rabbit checked by your veterinarian, because pain can make an animal vicious. If the vet finds nothing wrong, he can refer you to a qualified pet behaviourist, who can work with you to find a solution.

LITTER PROBLEMS

If your rabbit is urinating just outside the litter tray, the most likely reason is that the litter tray is too small or too shallow, and your bunny is simply missing the edge. Other causes include:

• Urinary infections
• A dislike of using a dirty tray
• The tray being too clean and having lost the right scent
• An older, stiff bunny who is reluctant to leap into a high tray
• Simply a mistake.

Try changing the tray (but keep the same type of litter) and your tray-cleaning routine, and put the tray on newspapers or a piece of plastic carpet protector.

If your rabbit starts to urinate or leave droppings in areas well away from his tray, ask yourself whether something has upset his routine. Maybe you have another bunny guest in the house, or perhaps you have moved his tray or changed the type of litter. This behaviour is absolutely normal when a new rabbit is introduced. It will stop once the new rabbit has bonded to the existing one.

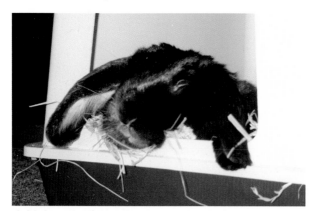

A high-entry litter tray is unsuitable for older bunnies, who may not be mobile enough to climb inside.

Litter trays should be clean – but not too clean!

GHOSTLY PRESENCE

A sudden change in her rabbit's character had owner Georgina Turner very concerned. Fortunately, it was all in her bunny's imagination…

"Smudge was my first houserabbit and I bought her when she was around eight weeks old. Even within the first few weeks, she was remarkably friendly, following me around the house and sitting by my feet, demanding that I stroke and fuss her. Within a few weeks, she was using her litter tray really well. In fact, she was such a neat, clean little rabbit that I was really amazed when I came down one morning to find she had shredded all the newspaper I used for lining the floor of her pen.

"When I went to let her out for her run, she growled at me and lunged forward, boxing at me with her front paws. She wasn't interested in coming out and I was really worried that she might be ill – I'd never seen her behave like this before.

"A few hours later she was running around with a great big mouthful of hay and scratching and digging away furiously in the bedroom compartment of her pen. When I peered in, she had built a big nest of shredded newspaper, hay and fur! I knew she couldn't be pregnant so I didn't understand why she was nesting. I phoned my best friend, who used to be a vet, and she explained that rabbits can have phantom pregnancies and that this was probably happening to Smudge.

"Over the next few months, Smudge had a few more phantom pregnancies. The day I came home from work to find her under the duvet on my bed constructing a beautiful nest from hay and mounds of her own fur was the day I decided to go ahead and have her spayed. I was concerned about the operation, but, as my vet had lots of experience with rabbits, I was reassured. Smudge was quiet for a few days after her operation, but she soon bounced back. She's never had another phantom pregnancy since and she seems much happier without these grumpy mood swings every few months."

Smudge – haunted by a phantom pregnancy.

Young rabbits may be a bit too easily distractible to remember to use their tray, and, in that case, it is worth putting a few extra trays down, one in every room plus any obvious problem areas. This should be temporary only!

The strategy to tackle most litter-training problems is to go back to basics. Put your rabbit (and his tray) back into a cage or small area and shut him in there for at least 48 to 72 hours, until he is reliably using his tray again.

In the meantime, thoroughly clean any soiled area with an enzymatic cleaner. This will prevent the smell from attracting the rabbit to toilet in the same place.

You can purchase special cleaners from pet shops. Alternatively, you can use a dilute solution of biological washing powder in warm water. Always patch test the fabric or carpet first. White wine vinegar is also useful for removing rabbit urine stains.

Urinating on furniture

It is not uncommon for houserabbits occasionally to urinate on sofas, beds, or other soft furniture impregnated with human scents.

Unfortunately, preventing this behaviour can be quite difficult. If you can, deny the rabbit access to the room he is soiling for a couple of weeks. This should help to prevent a pattern forming. If this is not possible, cage the rabbit temporarily while you go through the cleaning routines outlined above.

Once you are making progress and the rabbit is allowed to run about the room again, you must keep him off the furniture concerned, until he eventually grows out of the habit. This will probably require close supervision, as well as consistent retraining with the "No!" command.

If you stick to the rules of training outlined above, have your rabbit neutered, and don't expect too much from an adolescent

Furniture should be out of bounds when retraining a persistent offender!

rabbit, you and your houserabbit should sail through the 'bunny from hell' phase with ease. Very soon, you will have a delightful, mature, laid-back rabbit who is a pleasure to have around your home.

CHAPTER NINE

THE SOCIAL ANIMAL

Rabbits are social animals and they need company. They can form a close bond with other rabbits and with their human owners, but they are also capable of forming friendships with other animal species, such as dogs and cats.

Most houserabbit owners have to cope with either working long hours, looking after a home, or bringing up a human family – or a mixture of any number of human commitments. At some point, you may start to think about getting some company for your bunny. What is the best combination, and how can you safely mix rabbits with other pets and young children?

KEEPING TWO RABBITS

For your rabbit, the benefits of having a bunny companion are unquestionable. A bonded pair of rabbits provide one another with constant companionship in the most natural way; remember that wild rabbits live in groups. For you, having two bunnies will relieve you of some of the responsibility of keeping your rabbit company for several hours a day.

However, be prepared for your rabbit to become less attached to you and more attached to his bunny friend. The pleasure of watching a bonded pair of rabbits interacting with each other should more than compensate for any reduction in the intensity of your relationship with your existing rabbit.

Introducing a new rabbit is not as straightforward as you might think. Although rabbits are gregarious animals, they are also very territorial, and the resident rabbit will have to learn to accept the newcomer. Early introductions can be somewhat fraught, and it often takes a few weeks before the pair of rabbits will live together happily. Adjusting to life with a new partner is stressful to both rabbits, and care needs to be taken if one or both of them has any chronic health problems. Also, don't forget that there is usually a temporary loss of litter-training during the introduction period, so there will be more mess. You will also need to double your budget for veterinary care and bunny running costs!

Possible pairings

The first thing to say is that, unless you are starting off with baby rabbits, both parties must be neutered.

Rabbits enjoy the company of other bunnies.

The easiest pairing is introducing a new female to a resident male. Most male rabbits are quite happy to welcome a new lady friend to their abode. Female rabbits are usually more territorial than males and you will need to watch for outbreaks of aggression if you introduce a male into the home of a resident female. However, serious problems are unusual.

Same-sex pairings, such as female/female and particularly male/male, can be very difficult to establish. Unless you have two rabbits you particularly want to live together, you would be well advised to stick to opposite-sex pairings. If you proceed with a same-sex pairing, you must be prepared for a prolonged bonding period. This may extend to months, rather than weeks, if the rabbits dislike each other at first meeting.

Siblings

Starting out with two baby rabbits from the same litter is another option. Although the rabbits will have none of the problems that can be associated with introducing older bunnies, there are drawbacks to this arrangement.

Firstly, as the rabbits are already bonded with each other, it will be difficult for you to establish a relationship with either. Secondly, they will both enter puberty at about the same time. You will have to cope with two 'bunnies from hell' simultaneously, plus the expense and stress of having two rabbits neutered at the same time.

If you choose siblings, careful timing of their neutering operations is essential. Two brothers must be neutered as soon as their testicles descend and before they start fighting. Even so, this does not guarantee they will continue to live together happily. The pairing may be easily upset – by the presence or scent of a female rabbit, for example – and, if things go wrong, re-introduction may prove impossible.

Two sisters can make lovely companions, providing they are both spayed at sexual maturity. A brother/sister pair has the potential to get along very well, but you must take great care to avoid an accidental pregnancy. If you are confident that you will recognise when the male's testicles have descended and have him neutered immediately, the two can stay together continuously. This is because male rabbits become fertile a few weeks before females. Otherwise, you will have to separate the rabbits temporarily, before the male becomes fertile and for at least a couple of weeks post-castration. Ensure the rabbits can see and smell one another during this time.

Keeping two siblings may compromise an owner's relationship with the animals.

A rescue centre is a good place to find a companion for your houserabbit.

Finding your second rabbit

A specialist rescue centre is the best place to begin your search for your rabbit's new mate. Some rescue centres vaccinate and neuter rabbits prior to offering them for adoption, and many have volunteer staff with expertise in pairing rabbits. You may be able to take your rabbit along with you to choose his own mate. Ring the centre first, to see if they have space available for a neutral-territory meeting between the rabbits. Finding a 'love at first sight' companion in this manner is usually a very reliable method of ensuring the rabbits are compatible. However, if things don't work out subsequently, you should be able to take the new rabbit back.

Purchasing your second rabbit from a pet shop has none of these advantages and incorrect sexing of rabbits is remarkably common. If you have a particular breed of rabbit in mind, contact a reputable breeder. While few breeders can offer expertise in pairing rabbits, your new bunny should be accurately sexed, well handled, and healthy. Some breeders are willing to arrange for an adult rabbit to be neutered before you pick it up, and most would take the rabbit back if insurmountable problems arose.

Introductions

It is possible to find rabbits who will fall madly in love, snuggling up and grooming one another straight away. They can be left to get on with it. Other pairings will need some input from you, to help things run smoothly. The introduction process must not be hurried, and may take several weeks.

The first stage in getting your resident rabbit used to the newcomer without any conflict is to put the new bunny in a cage and allow physical contact. The easiest way to do this is for your existing rabbit to approach and sniff him or her through the wires. If your existing rabbit is free-range, put the cage in the room where he sleeps. If he is still caged when unsupervised, put the cages side by side. Over a few days, the rabbits will become accustomed to each other's smell. You could hasten this process by swapping their litter trays over, but this may have an adverse effect on litter-training.

The second stage is closely supervised contact on strictly neutral territory, possibly a kitchen or bathroom, to which the resident rabbit normally has no access. Furnish the area with some distractions, like cardboard boxes and tunnels, so the rabbits have a choice of activity other than confronting each other.

When the rabbits first meet, some chasing and mounting behaviour is absolutely normal, even if both are neutered. There may even be the odd nip, with a bit of fur pulled out. If tensions rise beyond this level, stop the session and separate the bunnies – the goal is to increase acceptance, not to teach them to fight. Don't let a full-blown fight develop. Fighting rabbits can inflict terrible injuries on one another and there is simply no need to put either animal through the stress of fighting his or her corner.

Often, the rabbits tolerate each other for only a few minutes before getting wound up. If this

Placing the cages nearer to each other over a period of time will help the rabbits to get used to each other – without feeling threatened.

occurs, put both bunnies in one large box on the back seat of the car, and take them for a car ride. Travelling by car is a bit scary, and the rabbits will be busy keeping their balance, which means that they can't adopt aggressive body language. Once you get back from the drive, split the pair up immediately. Every time you take them for a ride, leave them together longer and longer. Then return them to the neutral territory and try again.

Once these sessions in neutral territory are going well, gradually increase their duration, and possibly try feeding the rabbits together. It is a good sign if the rabbits ignore one another; and it is better still if they are prepared to lie together. You should now move the sessions to the resident rabbit's territory.

Do not hurry any stage. It is much quicker in the long run to build up things gradually, rather than risking a

major scrap and a return to square one. Once the rabbits are willing to sit together in the resident rabbit's territory, they are ready to be left together all the time.

As you can imagine, it is much easier and quicker to start off with a pair of rabbits who show immediate signs of accepting each other. Rabbits who ignore one another, groom themselves in the presence of the other rabbit, or groom the other bunny, show signs of acceptance. Persuading rabbits who initially fight to live together is not impossible, but it can take an awfully long time.

Grooming in the presence of another rabbit is a sure sign of acceptance.

NEW BUNNY ON THE BLOCK

Helen Flack has successfully introduced successive houserabbits, and has learnt a great deal from past mistakes.

"Ever since I had my first houserabbit, Bugsie, I have always kept a pair of rabbits together. As a single, career girl, working long hours and odd shifts, it was not fair to leave my devoted companion on her own for long periods of time.

"My first attempt at finding Bugsie a mate was almost a disaster, due to my ignorance at the time. The only information I could find about keeping rabbits together was in an old-fashioned pet book, which stated that you should not keep two males together. I wrongly assumed it would be all right to get another female.

"The initial meeting was horrendous. Chasing, biting, fur flying – poor Bugsie only escaped because she could climb the stairs and Blufa, the new rabbit, hadn't yet learned this skill! Not knowing what to do, I left them to it. I now know how lucky I was that neither of them sustained a serious injury. However, due to the fact that they had lots of space and hiding places, eventually they settled down. It wasn't what I had intended, though. It was really stressful – for them and me – and I would never recommend anyone leaving two rabbits to sort it out like this.

"A few years later, Blufa died. Bugs found her second mate by chance. I had taken on a baby bunny called Bita, who had eye problems. As Bita was so poorly and needed constant attention, I had him in a cage in the living room. Bugs got used to having him there, and, apart from leaving a load of droppings outside his cage, she seemed quite happy to tolerate him. Eventually, as he got fitter and after he had been neutered, I started to let him hop out when Bugsie was out of the room. Finally,

Bita and Cleo – love at first sniff!

wary of what had happened with Blufa, I decided to introduce them in the kitchen, as this was territory belonging to neither.

"The initial meeting was fine, with just a bit of chasing and sniffing. Soon they were firm friends, spending their entire time together grooming one another and lying on my bed. Bugsie and Bita became inseparable, and, as Bita was nearly completely blind, I felt he relied very much on his rabbit companion. Bugsie was quite an old lady by this time, and, throughout the last months of her life, she was too stiff to manage the stairs. Maybe because his eyesight deteriorated further, Bita never climbed the stairs either and spent all his time downstairs with Bugsie.

"When Bugs passed away, I'm sure Bita was pining. He started climbing upstairs again on the day she died, and wouldn't leave the bed where he used to sit with his mate.

"Obviously, I had to find him another friend. This time I took him to a rescue centre to see if we could find the perfect match. We put him in an empty run while I went to look at the rabbits available. The first two that I liked were not going to work. The first one chased him round trying to bite his bottom. The second he lunged at, and she ran, terrified, to her hutch and refused to come out.

"Then we tried the sister of this timid bunny and it was completely different. Initially, they ignored each other. Next, Bita started grooming himself while she nibbled at the grass. Eventually, they hopped over to one another; the little girl put her head down and Bita started to lick her ears. That was it. She travelled home together with him in his carrying box, and, as soon as she hopped out into the house, she went straight to his litter tray and used it. From that day forwards, Bita and Cleo were perfect companions – love at first sniff!"

RABBIT AND GUINEA PIG

Never buy a guinea pig thinking it will be an easier or cheaper companion for your bunny than another rabbit. It is easy to forget that rabbits and guinea pigs are very different species, with differing physical and behavioural needs

Many houserabbit owners are aiming for a free-range bunny. If you have a guinea pig, this may not be possible, as litter-training guinea pigs is much more difficult than training rabbits, and it usually entails multiple shallow litter trays round the edges of every room.

There are also specific health issues to consider. Rabbits may carry a bacterium called *Bordetella bronchiseptica*, which is hazardous to guinea pigs. The two species have different dietary requirements too. Guinea pigs cannot synthesise their own vitamin C and must obtain it from their diet, necessitating the feeding of fresh greens. This is not a problem if your rabbit is eating a hay-and-vegetable diet, but it is a consideration if he's not.

While there are many cases where a rabbit/guinea pig pair has worked well, unfortunately, there are many other examples where this pairing has been disastrous for one or both

Although guinea pigs and rabbits are often kept together, they are not ideally suited as companions.

animals. It is usually the guinea pig that comes off worst – a kick from a rabbit can seriously injure a guinea pig, and, if the rabbit starts to mount the guinea pig, the pig may be badly bitten and will certainly be frightened. There are also cases of guinea pigs biting rabbits, resulting in serious problems with abscesses.

Keeping rabbits and guinea pigs together is not recommended, although if you already have pair living together happily, don't split them up! If you are determined to try it, bear in mind that, if things don't work out, you will have two lonely animals rather than one. Make sure the rabbit is neutered and male guinea pigs are castrated. The guinea pig must be provided with a safe refuge, such as a small drainpipe, that the rabbit cannot get into. Above all, you must be constantly alert for problems.

PREDATORS OR PALS?

Rabbits are prey animals; dogs and cats are predators. Can it ever be safe to allow a rabbit to live with an animal that is programmed to regard it as dinner? In practice, it does not appear to be a problem. Rabbits and cats may end up being best of friends, and many people have a happy household, with their rabbit sharing the hearthrug with a dog. However, it's not always possible and it's not always plain sailing.

DOGS

The likelihood of a successful canine/rabbit combination is largely determined by the personality of the dog and his degree of socialisation and training. Some breeds, with a highly developed chase instinct (e.g. terriers and sighthounds), may not be able to restrain themselves if the rabbit makes a sudden move.

However, animal behaviourists now recognise that breed is less important than socialisation, and whether or not the dog has met rabbits or cats during the critical socialisation period between three and twelve weeks of age.

Before contemplating mixing a rabbit with a dog, you need to consider practical matters, as well as preparing a contingency plan in case the introductions don't work out. For example, in an open-plan home, you would find it difficult to separate your animals when you are unable to supervise them. Even if one of the pets were caged, the other could easily tease or terrify the caged party.

Safety First

For the majority of people, introducing a rabbit and dog will take considerable effort and time. How you go about introducing rabbit to dog will depend on whether it's the dog or the rabbit who is already in residence!

If your starting point is a resident dog, prepare for the arrival of the rabbit well in advance. If the dog is young or not yet trained, wait until he is more mature. Teach your dog

the commands "No!", "Leave", and "Gentle". Reward him for calmly passing cats on walks, and don't encourage him to chase wild rabbits. Clicker-training your dog will make it easier for you to teach him acceptable behaviour around your rabbit. It is also a good idea to train your dog to wear a muzzle. If you put it on at completely random times, such as when you are watching television, the dog will learn to accept it in the same way that he accepts his collar. It is important to get your dog used to the muzzle before you introduce the rabbit, otherwise he will associate the muzzle with exciting, small furry creatures. The initial introduction can then be made with the dog muzzled, which enhances safety and helps you to be relaxed, which, in turn, keeps the dog calm.

If you already have a houserabbit, it's worth taking care to choose the right dog. If you can find an adult dog that is already used to living alongside rabbits or cats, you will be halfway there. If you want a puppy, you will be able to ensure that he meets rabbits within the socialisation period, but it might be months until he is calm and restrained enough to be able to run around with the rabbit.

Introductions

When the day comes to introduce the animals, put the dog on a lead and the rabbit in his cage. Your dog is likely to be fascinated by this strange new creature – he may pull on the lead, sniff hard, wag his tail or get into the 'play bow' position. Be ready to use the "Off" or "Leave" command, and reward the dog for calm, relaxed behaviour.

Sighthounds, such as this Lurcher, have traditionally hunted rabbits – but breed instincts can be tempered with early training and socialisation.

CANINE COMMOTIONS

Rachel and Gary Todd have two houserabbits and two dogs. Unfortunately, they don't all mix. Rachel explains how she worked things out…

"We started off with just the rabbits – Cerys and Louie. Then, we moved to a larger house and our circumstances finally allowed us to adopt a dog. Along came Vader, a Dobermann-cross, who eventually settled down well with the rabbits and liked to sprawl out on the rug beside them. However, when we later adopted a second dog, things got a bit more complicated.

"The new dog, a spaniel called Obi, would lunge at the rabbits, and get so excited he would wet all over the floor! At this stage, the rabbits were based in the utility room. Obi's arrival meant they could no longer come and play in the living room unless Obi was elsewhere or wearing his headcollar. We decided to move the rabbits into a spare double bedroom, and the extra space would compensate for the loss of access to the living room and kitchen.

"Twelve months on, Obi still can't be trusted around the rabbits, and he is liable to chase them. Sadly, Louie died, and we are introducing Cerys to her new mate, Malcolm. We have to set aside quality time to spend in the rabbits' room, but we manage to give all the animals enough attention. Having said this, I can't deny that it is very different from our original plan of having all the animals together with us in the living room every evening. If we hadn't had the facilities to come up with the solution we have, we would not have contemplated even trying to take on a dog."

Launching at the rabbit is not a good sign. You may be able to deter this with the "Off" command, or with a squirt from a water pistol, but too much excitement is not a good idea, and you should interrupt the session and allow the dog to calm down. Never chastise or punish the dog for showing interest in the rabbit. Reward desired behaviour instead, otherwise the dog may start to resent the rabbit, leading to a potentially dangerous situation later on.

Hopefully, the dog will gradually lose interest in the caged bunny. Start again, with the dog on the lead (and preferably muzzled), and this time allow the rabbit to come out of the cage. Over time, the dog can come off the lead with the rabbit loose in the room.

If, however, the dog continues to launch himself at the caged rabbit, then you will have to decide whether to persevere. The dog must relax in the presence of the rabbit, and, if this cannot be achieved, you will never be able to have both animals loose in the same room. As it would be unfair to keep your rabbit permanently caged, unless you can keep the animals completely separated and provide both with enough attention, then it may be best to have one of them rehomed. Before taking this drastic step, consider obtaining professional advice from a qualified pet behaviour counsellor.

However well you think your dog and rabbit are getting along, always remember that one mistake could prove fatal for your rabbit. Dogs are programmed to move suddenly and swiftly in response to movement. The safest advice is never to leave your dog and rabbit together unsupervised, and certainly not for prolonged periods of time.

CATS
Although cats are natural predators of rabbits, this combination is remarkably successful, with introductions being more straightforward than those with dogs.

One factor that facilitates cat/rabbit friendships is the complementary body language of the two species. A dominant rabbit may push

INTRODUCING DOGS AND RABBITS

Initially, the dog will show interest in the newcomer.

It is important that the dog is restrained when face-to-face introductions are attempted.

Over several supervised introductions, the novelty will soon wear off, and the dog is likely to become more interested in the rabbit's food or bed than the bunny itself!

Mutual grooming is a sure sign of firm friendship.

FRIENDLY PHOEBE

With time and careful handling, dogs and bunnies can be friends – as Cathy Brown can testify.

"I spent ages looking for the right dog. With two houserabbits already in residence, my wish-list of canine attributes was very long indeed. I needed a bitch that was good with kids, dogs, and cats. She had to be house-trained, good in the car, used to being left, and short-coated. As I trekked around various dogs' homes every weekend, anyone would have thought I was seeking a flying pig!

"In the end, I heard about the perfect dog completely by chance – someone wanted a new home for a 10-month-old crossbreed, as they were finding it difficult to cope with her exercise requirements as well as two young children. I brought Phoebe home on trial a few weeks later. My rabbits have the run of the house, so it was Phoebe who went into a cage – a nice, big puppy pen. She was remarkably good, and she would lie on her duvet watching the rabbits intently, but with no whining or leaping about.

"Taking her through the kitchen in order to reach the back garden was another matter. Even on a lead, she invariably tried to bound up to the rabbits. It was at least a month before she started to lose interest in them, and, during this time, I have to admit, I was starting to have doubts whether it would work out. Things improved once she realised that rabbit droppings were tasty treats, and her attention diverted to the litter tray when we passed through the kitchen!

"The next stage was to have a rabbit on my lap and Phoebe on the floor, or vice versa. She was allowed to sniff and lick them gently, but, for a long time, I was very wary of her worrying interest in nibbling the backs of their necks. We're at the stage now where the rabbits and Phoebe can run around together in the same room. Phoebe isn't allowed to play chase games with her ball if the rabbits are in the room – I encourage her to lie quietly on her bed and chew a bone. Occasionally, the two rabbits will lie down beside the dog on the rug, which is really sweet, and, if we're in the kitchen, Phoebe loves to sit on the rabbit's bed with her back pressed against the radiator. I will leave them together if I nip upstairs to the bathroom, or into the kitchen, but that's the limit.

"Phoebe chases wild rabbits, and she got very excited when we visited a friend who also has a houserabbit. She's fine with her own rabbit family, but anyone else's needs to watch out! It's a bit like the comments you see in dog magazines – 'fine with own cats, chases others'.

"I've no regrets about bringing a dog into a household with rabbits already in residence. The bunnies have shown nothing but benign curiosity in the dog, and they certainly don't seem worried or upset by her. However, I knew that success was not guaranteed, and, when I adopted Phoebe, it was on the understanding that, if I couldn't make it work, she could go back to her old family to await another new mum."

his head under the cat's chin, 'presenting' in order to demand a lick. With cats, it is the dominant one doing the grooming so, when a cat grooms a rabbit, each animal happily believes they are the boss!

The best strategy if you want a houserabbit and a cat to live alongside one another is to choose a large bunny. You need to be cautious if your rabbit is a dwarf breed and the cat is a hunter. You will probably find that the rabbit prefers not to use the same litter tray as the cat.

Introductions

The process of introducing cats and rabbits is similar to that outlined for dogs and rabbits. You should make the first introductions with one of the animals in a cage. As with dogs, the cat should be rewarded for displaying calm behaviour around the bunny, and she should learn to associate the presence of the rabbit with pleasant things. For example, you could feed your cat next to the rabbit. It also helps if the cat is familiar with the smell of the rabbit. Transfer the scent of the rabbit to the cat by stroking both animals with a cloth, in turn.

Once cat and rabbit are relaxed, you can start to let them out together. Close supervision will be essential at first, but it shouldn't take long for the two to settle down and become firm friends.

There are many cases of houserabbits and cats who have developed such a strong bond that they groom each other, and sleep and play together, although this shouldn't be allowed until your cat has learned to keep her claws retracted.

When you are sure that cat and rabbit are best buddies, you can leave them together all the time. However, this could take time, and, until then, separate them when you are not around to supervise.

RABBITS AND CHILDREN

So, it is possible for rabbits to live safely with two of their predators, cats and dogs, but what about combining rabbits with children? Having children does not preclude having a houserabbit, and there is certainly no need to rehome your rabbit if you are expecting your first child. However, you will need to take extra care to ensure that your bunny does not get overlooked, and there are safety issues that need addressing for the benefit of both the rabbit and the child.

The rabbit is the most vulnerable of the two and you must ensure that children neither hurt nor frighten the rabbit. Even normal childish behaviour, such as shouting, crying, and falling over, can be terrifying to a rabbit, especially if a toddler tries to chase the rabbit.

Cats and rabbits use similar body language, so often learn to communicate well with each other.

Caroline Field, from London, describes how her feline family adopted a bunny interloper.

"We work from home and we felt we could adequately supervise our three cats when we added a baby rabbit into the equation. For the first couple of weeks, we kept the rabbit in a cage. Whenever we handled her, we involved the cats and cuddled them at the same time, so no one's nose would be put out of joint and they'd all learn how to interact with one another.

"Astonishingly, they got on extremely well and never displayed any antipathy nor aggression. If anything, the cats were slightly alarmed by the way the rabbit hopped about, but they quickly got used to this. Soon we were sufficiently confident to end the rabbit's confinement. Although she continued to eat and go to the loo in the old cage, she chose a sofa as her main base, and, from there, she ruled the roost. Gradually, she allowed the cats to join her on the sofa, and soon they all took to snuggling up together. Only very rarely was there a disagreement between them – usually about who got the box of hay to sleep in – but it would be quickly resolved and was never violent.

"A few months later, we rescued a badly neglected kitten from a pet shop. The rabbit immediately took him under her wing, and, on balance, probably played a greater part in his recuperation and upbringing than we did. She was an excellent surrogate mother and the kitten grew up well adjusted and healthy, which was nothing short of miraculous given the state he'd been in when he joined us.

"When our rabbit died suddenly, at only three years old, we were miserable and the cats were miserable. They mourned her death just as they had one of their own, a few months previously.

"I wouldn't hesitate to bring another rabbit into our set-up in the future, but I would stress that our cats are not hunters, nor are they aggressive towards one another. Anyone else considering introducing houserabbits into a cat household would have to consider the temperaments of all the animals concerned. You need to decide – objectively – whether cat and rabbit will get on before attempting to bring them together. Realistically, you should also prepare a back-up plan, in case there is any trouble and any of the animals' welfare is put at risk by the new arrangement.

"You should be willing to give all the animals a great deal of time and atttention, especially while they integrate with one another. It is also essential that you have enough space for the new addition, so that cats' territories are not disturbed by the 'interloper', who will also need to establish his or her own territory."

All rabbits need a burrow substitute, and this is especially so in a household containing children. This surrogate burrow is usually the rabbit's cage, and it must be inaccessible to the kids.

If your child can understand that the cage is 'out of bounds', fine, but, if you have a baby or toddler, you will need to arrange the cage so that the rabbit can get in but the child cannot. This may be as simple as facing the door of the cage towards a wall, which will allow only a bunny-sized gap.

Introductions

Teach your children to sit quietly on the floor, allowing the rabbit to initiate contact. You could make a game out of this, with the whole family sitting in a circle, rabbit in the middle, and seeing who the bunny 'talks to' next. It's worth teaching small children to stroke the rabbit using the back of their hand – this way they are far less likely to accidentally hit the bunny. Given time, you will find that the rabbit will become relaxed in the presence of the children and you may even find the bunny sprawled out

All interactions between rabbits and children should be at ground level.

on the floor alongside the kids.

It is vitally important that children are never allowed to pick up the rabbit. If the rabbit is dropped, he may be severely injured, and, if the rabbit feels at all insecure, he will struggle and possibly scratch or bite the child. Even if a child picks up a rabbit confidently and with perfect technique, small hands inevitably dig in and this will be uncomfortable for the bunny. Leave all rabbit/child interactions at ground level and everyone will be much happier and safer.

Even if you have no children of your own, it is worth having a cage available for use during visits from friends' and relatives' kids. Your rabbit will not be accustomed to these strange, small humans with their peculiar smells and noises, and may not be very impressed, preferring peace and quiet.

FACING FAILURE

Although you hope it will never happen, there may come a time when you have to consider parting with your houserabbit.

There are many factors that can affect our lives. A job may mean a move abroad; a relationship may break up; or an unexpected illness may strike, any of which may mean that you cannot give your rabbit the time and attention you anticipated. Very occasionally, the rabbit is the problem.

Maybe he simply will not settle as an indoor rabbit, or it simply isn't working out between him and the rest of your pets. Faced with any of these scenarios, you are likely to feel upset or even guilty that you have let your rabbit down, which is entirely understandable.

You will probably want to explore every possible avenue before parting with your rabbit, but, if no solution can be found, you will have to find him a loving new home.

Finding the right home may not be easy, and you should do everything possible to make your rabbit as adoptable as possible. If he's not already neutered and vaccinated, arrange for this to be done. Your local houserabbit association

Rescued rabbits soon adapt to their new homes, and, with the right handling, can settle in very quickly.

ANIMAL HOUSE

Miranda and Mark Dickinson, from Northumberland, brought up their sons Richard (11) and Charlie (7) alongside a selection of animals. They currently have one dog (a Lurcher) and two houserabbits. Miranda tells how she achieved multi-species harmony.

"I have always had pets in the house and I was determined that having children would not change this. We have worked our way through the usual succession of indoor pets, from hamsters through to dogs, but the rabbits only moved indoors a couple of years ago.

"When the boys were tiny, they weren't allowed to play with any of the small animals, although they were allowed to play with the dog under supervision. As they got older, and learnt more restraint, they were allowed more interaction with the various pets. By the time Charlie was five, his heart was set on a rabbit of his own. I really fancied having a houserabbit, so we decided to go ahead. A friend of the family bred Polish rabbits, a lively, miniature breed some people would say are completely unsuitable as pets, but we fell in love with these cheeky little bunnies and had to have

Bouncer – by name and by nature.

one. The entire litter came to live here temporarily, to become socialised with children and dogs, and to generally become accustomed to family life. When the rest of the litter went off to their new homes, we kept a little black buck, Bouncer.

"Initially, Bouncer lived in a hutch in the utility room. We made a rule that the kids were not allowed to pick him up. If they wanted to play with him, they took a box to his hutch, opened the door, and let him choose whether he wanted to jump into the box. Once in the box, he could be safely carried to the living room, where he was allowed to run all over the children. They weren't allowed to grab him or try to hold him.

"Three years later, Bouncer is neutered and running loose in the house. The boys still don't pick him up. He's not a cuddly rabbit and he doesn't like to be held, but he is confident around the boys. If they sit or lie on the floor, he will clamber fearlessly all over them, and he loves to sit on their shoulders. He doesn't like to be stroked, except by Charlie, to whom he presents and demands nose-rubs! I think it's because Charlie is the one person whom he trusts totally, because he has never picked him up!"

may be able to offer advice and support, and you should contact all the rabbit rescues within reasonable distance – they may have someone looking for a houserabbit and be able to put you in direct contact with a potential new owner. If at all possible, hang on to your rabbit and find a home for him directly. Then he doesn't have to

go through the upheaval of going to a rescue centre before being rehomed from there.

Finally, do not make the mistake of thinking you are the only person who loves rabbits. You may be heartbroken at parting with your companion, but he might just change someone else's life for the better.

A FOND FAREWELL

Tessa Evans, from North Wales, parted with her New Zealand White rabbit, Amy, six months ago. Here, she explains why she made the difficult decision to rehome Amy.

"I adopted Amy from the university lab animal department, all legal and above board, three years ago. She was spayed and vaccinated before I got her.

"As a lab rabbit, she used to jump out of her pen away from the other rabbits in the group, so I guess I should have realised she was a bit of a loner. I wanted her to bond with my existing pair of houserabbits, but it just didn't work. So poor Amy spent all her time in my study. She had the run of the room, but she was definitely lonely.

"My time was spread too thinly, trying to spend quality time with an upstairs rabbit as well as a downstairs pair, and I should have admitted then that things weren't working. I think I was ashamed to admit that, although I had adopted Amy fully intending to look after her for life, I couldn't make it work.

"When I was studying for postgraduate exams, and spending hours in the study, Amy was in heaven. She's a real cuddle-bun, and she would lie across my feet, climb half into my lap, and generally lap up the attention.

"When I went on holiday, some friends of mine offered to look after her for me. They had two children, and I knew they were looking for a large rabbit. When I got back from holiday, I went to collect Amy.

"She was so happy she looked like a pig in muck. In fact, she had such a good time playing in the garden that she could have been a pig in muck – she was black! She was relaxed, she was happy, and she was almost throwing herself at the children for attention. She played out during the day, coming into the house at night and sleeping in the children's beds. There was no way she was coming back to a life of boredom in my study.

"I still see her regularly. She recognises me and bounds up to have her nose rubbed. When I see her lying down, relaxing by the fire with her new family, I sometimes think what might have been, but there is no doubt in my mind that she is much, much happier now.

"I only wish I had come to a decision after a few months rather than two and a half years. But then I might not have stumbled upon the perfect home for her, so I suppose it was fate."

Amy: lonely and bored, a new home was the kindest option.

CHAPTER TEN

FUN TIME

ouserabbits are addictive. After sharing your home with a rabbit for a few months, you may well find yourself wanting to link up with other rabbit enthusiasts to learn more about rabbit care and behaviour, or helping rabbits less fortunate than yours. There are many ways of doing this and perhaps the first step would be to join a rabbit club or association.

NETWORKING

There are national houserabbit organisations in several countries including the UK and the US.

In the US, the House Rabbit Society (HRS) is a rescue and welfare organisation, helping unwanted and cruelty-case rabbits. Rabbits are fostered in expert foster homes, organised by chapters that are present in many states. Most of these chapters produce a newsletter, and the national organisation also publishes a magazine. The HRS has a strong Internet presence and maintains an excellent rabbit website.

In the UK, the main club for pet rabbit owners is now the Rabbit Welfare Association (RWA), having, in January 2002, incorporated the British Houserabbit Association (BHRA). It welcomes all rabbit lovers, with a special emphasis on supporting people whose rabbits live indoors. Membership provides many benefits, including an extremely popular quarterly magazine, social events, and educational conferences, as well as access to a network of advisors to assist with rabbit problems. It maintains a list of nationwide 'rabbit-friendly' vets and welcomes members from around the globe.

In addition, the RWA aims to educate and inform the public, pet industry and veterinary profession, about the true natures and needs of the domestic rabbit, through its Rabbit Welfare Fund. The fund produces a range of leaflets, as well as funding research into rabbit welfare issues. Individual association members support the Rabbit Welfare Fund via their subscriptions and donations.

Perhaps the Internet, more than anything else, has been responsible for triggering and supporting the growth in houserabbit awareness. You will find numerous web sites relating to companion rabbits, complemented by a large number of mailing lists and discussion groups where you can 'talk rabbit' with other enthusiasts to your heart's content.

Internet guidelines

If you've never joined an e-mail discussion list before, you will be astonished at the variety and vigour of these Internet communities. Some of them (particularly those linked to associations like the RWA or the HRS) enable you to talk directly to national and international rabbit experts.

Some lists are strictly moderated, to ensure that discussion is confined to issues pertaining to health and welfare.

Others are more chatty and fun. Traffic levels vary too – the busiest lists may receive 200 messages a day. The lists vary in their outlook, with some having a middle-of-the-road stance and others leaning towards the animal rights movement. You need to choose a list where you feel comfortable, so sign up to a few and simply listen in for a few days before joining in.

When you first sign up for a list, you'll be sent some information outlining the rules of the list and an indication of what topics may and may not be discussed. If the list is 'moderated', all contributions are screened before being released to other list members, which helps to keep the list 'on topic'. Unmoderated lists occasionally degenerate into squabbles ('flame wars'), so beginners are advised to stick to moderated lists.

If you are new to a list, always find out if there are any 'Frequently Asked Questions' (FAQs) available before posting a question to the entire list.

SHOWING

Exhibiting rabbits dates back to the 19th century. Although this hobby is now declining in popularity from its heyday in the last century, rabbit breeders (known as 'fanciers') have developed dozens of different breeds of rabbit over the years and the huge choice available today is due to the existence of the rabbit fancy.

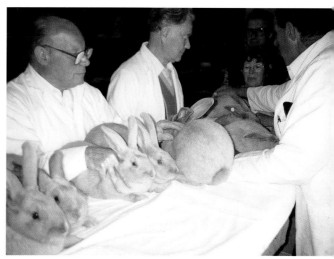

Houserabbits can enter fun events, but showing can never become a serious hobby, as neutered animals cannot be exhibited.

Anyone wanting to get a real idea of the enormous variety of different rabbit breeds and colours should try to visit a rabbit show. Many communities host social rabbit shows, which are held most weekends, often in village halls and community centres, with larger championship shows occurring every few months. In the summer, a large number of agricultural shows host a rabbit section.

There are limited opportunities for non-pedigree pet rabbits to participate in shows. Local clubs may put on pet classes. These are usually judged on condition, cleanliness and temperament, but often, these classes may be restricted to children's pets. To compete in the main show, the rabbit will be judged against a Breed Standard – a 'blueprint' of the ideal rabbit of a particular breed. To qualify for this, the rabbits must be pedigree.

In the UK, this means that the rabbit will have been fitted with a metal identification ring on a hind leg when it was young. The number on this ring will have been registered with the governing body of the UK rabbit fancy, the British Rabbit Council. Neutered rabbits cannot be exhibited, so this means that even many pedigree houserabbits are not eligible for shows.

BREEDING SHOW RABBITS

Keeping and breeding show rabbits is a fascinating hobby, but it is very different from keeping one or two houserabbits. Outside accommodation for multiple rabbits is required, and exhibitors have little choice but to cage their breeding animals individually, which, as we have already discussed, does not really cater for their physical and behavioural needs.

Potential fanciers must also decide how they would cope with the inevitable surplus produced in the quest to breed a show winner, or those who have grown too old to breed or exhibit. In bygone years, these animals would have fed the family, but this is now unacceptable to an increasing number of rabbit fanciers.

Finding caring permanent homes for a large number of young rabbits is not always easy. Many people feel that deliberately breeding more rabbits, when many thousands are unwanted every year, is unethical. However, the annual demand for pet rabbits vastly outstrips the numbers in rescue, so there is still an important role for breeders of high-quality, healthy pedigree stock.

Nevertheless, there are significant welfare and ethical problems within the rabbit fancy, which need to be addressed, and, as attitudes to rabbits change, it is to be hoped that, in the future, rabbit fanciers are prepared to tackle these concerns in an imaginative and open-minded manner.

Anyone interested in taking up exhibiting rabbits as a hobby should contact a local rabbit club, visit several shows, and discuss the hobby with experienced fanciers – possibly visiting an established rabbitry before making a decision.

Finding caring homes for baby bunnies is problematic, especially as there are already so many unwanted rabbits.

Photo shows raise money for good causes and give you the chance of sharing cute moments with fellow bunny lovers.

PHOTO SHOWS

In contrast to formal shows, postal photo shows can be enjoyed by any rabbit owner. Taking part in a postal photo show is great fun, and these events are often held in aid of rabbit welfare. Shows are usually advertised several weeks in advance by one of the rabbit organisations, and classes such as 'most appealing rabbit' and 'naughtiest rabbit' are listed. All you need to do is to send in the best, most appealing photograph you have of your rabbit.

SHOWJUMPING

Rabbit showjumping is a popular hobby in Scandinavia, but is little known in the UK or the US. Jumping rabbits wear a harness and lead, and jump over miniature versions of horse jumps. The best rabbits can clear 90 cm (3 ft) with ease.

Obviously, a showjumping rabbit needs to be fit and well handled. Training commences when the rabbit is at least four or five months old, and relies entirely upon rewarding the rabbit. Many

Rabbits love hopping around, and most take to showjumping with glee.

houserabbits are already accomplished jumpers (on to furniture and beds, for example), and it is not difficult to see that some rabbits would relish popping over a round of showjumps.

One point to bear in mind is that a rabbit who has spent all his life in a cage is likely to have thin, brittle bones due to lack of exercise. Please don't try to encourage an older rabbit you have recently adopted to jump.

THERAPY RABBITS

This is a most rewarding activity for you and your rabbit to become involved with. If you have a particularly laid-back bunny, who enjoys being handled and isn't upset by car travel, you may want to think about volunteering to visit hospitals and nursing homes with your rabbit. Therapy pet schemes have been dominated by dogs in the past, but rabbits can do just the same job, stimulating and interesting people who may be unwell, depressed, bored, or lonely in an institutional setting.

One UK organisation, the Children and Hospital and Animal Therapy Association (CHATA) has a number of rabbits on the

Therapy rabbits are becoming increasingly popular in hospitals.

books, visiting paediatric wards in hospitals with great success. It is an idea that could well be expanded to many other countries.

RABBIT RESCUE

While rabbits tend to be the third most popular pet, coming behind dogs and cats, unfortunately, they are also the most likely to be neglected. Thousands of unwanted rabbits pass through the rescue systems every year, and it is only natural that many rabbit lovers feel compelled to try to do something to alleviate this sad situation.

Hands-on work rescuing rabbits is only one part of the story. It can only ever pick up the pieces. Tackling the root causes of the unwanted rabbit problem requires a multi-faceted approach, including education of owners as well as changing the public perception of rabbits. The aim is to try to prevent rabbits from becoming unwanted in the first place. However, despite the best efforts of many, the lives of thousands of rabbits depend upon volunteers willing to give some time or money to help rescue, rehabilitate and rehome them.

Rescue rabbits are cared for in a variety of situations. Animal homes (run by large charities as well as independent shelters) usually accept rabbits as well as dogs and cats, and enthusiastic volunteers can make an enormous difference to rabbits in these facilities.

However, the majority of rabbits passing through rescue are handled in one of the hundreds of specialist centres across the country. Most are run by private individuals who have turned their garden into accommodation for anything from 10 to 200 rabbits. The best of these centres do a fantastic job rehoming large numbers of rabbits, as well as having the expertise to help 'problem rabbits' that arrive on the doorstep. If you are keen to support rabbit

GENTLE JADE

Anne Mitchell from West Sussex is so proud of her Cashmere Lop, Jade, she just loves sharing her with others!

"I've been taking Jade on visits for a while now. She's a beautiful rabbit, with long, soft fur, and she always provokes a comment from even the quietest patient. We visit the rehabilitation ward for elderly patients in our local hospital.

"Jade is really popular with the folk there. Because she is such a gentle, quiet bunny, she will sit quite happily for ages while the patients stroke her. I find the fact that she seems to perk them up very rewarding. Obviously, you have to be careful what sort of rabbit you take along on visits like these. Jade is ideal because she loves the attention and doesn't find the travelling or handling at all stressful. She is also a very clean bunny, so there have never been any accidents on the patients' beds! A lively youngster who won't sit still, who hates being handled or who isn't perfectly house-trained, would not work at all.

Anne Mitchell with Jade, a Cashmere Lop.

"Jade and I have also been along to a local day centre for the disabled, which provides rehabilitation activities for people with a range of physical disabilities.

"When I first took Jade to the centre, two of the blind visitors paid particular attention to her. The fact that Jade is so tactile, with her long coat and lovely warm ears, must have been what attracted them to her.

"I'm sure that there is a special bond between rabbits and the ill or elderly. Maybe it's the rabbit's vulnerability as a prey animal that the patients identify with, or it might just be that they remember rabbits as pets from their childhood, but everyone seems to find comfort in stroking the soft, warm fur of a living creature.

"The hospital staff recognise that Jade's visits are beneficial to the patients and have given us an open invitation to visit as often as we like. I find the visits very rewarding, and I'm hoping to arrange to take Jade into the children's hospice soon. I'm sure the kids will love her!"

Jade's long, soft fur and gentle temperament make her a big hit with hospital patients.

rescue, you might want to consider some of these practical ways to help.

• Adopt your next pet rabbit from a rescue centre and encourage others to do the same.
• Volunteer at your local rabbit rescue. There will always be hutches to be cleaned, but perhaps you could drop off or collect rabbits from the vet, collect bags of feed, take rubbish to the tip, or pop in to groom a rabbit or clip claws.
• Use your fundraising skills and hold a coffee morning or sponsored event to raise some much-needed cash.
• If you a keen DIY lover, you could help to refurbish donated hutches and runs that will be sold to support the rescues.
• If you have some spare space at home, you might be able to accept holiday boarding bunnies and donate the fees to the rescue. Alternatively, perhaps you have room for a spare hutch in the garden, to shelter a bunny temporarily if the main rescue is full. A spare fold-up puppy cage would enable you to shelter a homeless housebunny, which many shelters can't cater for.
• If you are good at PR, you could help raise the profile of rabbit rescue by contacting local newspapers and radio stations.
• If you only have a few hours to spare, you could animal-sit for a few hours or days, to enable the rescue centre owner to take a break.
• Financial support will always be welcome, however much or little.

Before pledging your support to any particular rabbit rescue, make sure you are happy with their conditions and their philosophy. It's reasonable to ask how your money will be spent.

Becoming involved in a rabbit rescue organisation is rewarding work.

Fostering

Fostering, where rabbit lovers accept one or two foster rabbits into their own home, has a strong tradition in American houserabbit circles. This system can help only a small percentage of unwanted rabbits, but those bunnies lucky enough to find a place benefit from a more thorough assessment and rehabilitation than is possible in most conventional rescue centres. Individual rabbit lovers sometimes take in an occasional unwanted rabbit; some rehome them, others accumulate a few unwanted bunnies and keep them for the rest of their lives.

Whatever the activities you decide to become involved in, you will find that meeting others who share your interest in these delightful animals will enrich your life.

Fostering enables the carer to make a thorough assessment, ensuring the rabbit will be suitably matched to his new owners.

CHAPTER ELEVEN

ACTIVE HEALTH CARE

The lifespan of the domestic rabbit is quite amazing when compared to wild rabbits, where life expectancy is typically less than two years. With good care and attention, and possibly a little luck, your houserabbit should live for seven to ten years or more – a few bunnies go on into their teens! Dwarf and small breeds tend to live the longest.

To maximise the chance of your rabbit living to a ripe old age, you must provide a healthy lifestyle, with lots of exercise, a balanced diet, and appropriate preventative health care. By and large, the infectious diseases that can wipe out breeding colonies of rabbits are unlikely to affect houserabbits, although there are two important exceptions – myxomatosis and VHD (see below).

In contrast, many of the health problems suffered by pampered pet rabbits are caused partially by poor diet. Obesity and related problems are particularly common, so it is important to pay attention to what your rabbit eats!

BREED PROBLEMS

Selective breeding of rabbits, as with other animals, can give rise to health problems. Some conditions are more common in certain breeds.

- Lops (Mini, Dwarf, Cashmere, French, German) and Netherland Dwarfs: Hereditary incisor malocclusion; dental and eye problems developing later in life.
- French Lops: Entropion.
- Rex: Sore hocks; respiratory infections.

The Rex can be prone to sore hocks and respiratory infection.

As prey animals, rabbits conceal any sign of illness so predators do not see them as an easy meal.

- Giant breeds: Short-lived in general; degenerative joint disease.
- Long-haired breeds: Flystrike; gut stasis.

RECOGNISING SYMPTOMS

Rabbits don't shout from the rooftops when they are ill or in pain. Early signs of ill health can be extremely subtle and easily missed. This is because rabbits are prey animals, programmed to conceal any outward signs of illness to avoid alerting potential predators to an easy meal.

Sadly, many pet rabbits suffer because of this behavioural trait. Rabbits living outdoors in hutches are particularly vulnerable; these animals are usually only visited once a day, and, by the time the rabbit is obviously ill, it is often too late for effective treatment. Thankfully, houserabbits get a much better deal.

As time passes, you will get to know your bunny so well that you will notice even a slight change in behaviour, enabling you to seek prompt veterinary attention. Of course, prevention is better than cure. It is worth establishing a regular routine of checking your rabbit, to make sure he stays in tip-top shape.

As well as these home health checks, rabbits (just like dogs and cats) need to visit the vet at least once a year for their vaccinations. This annual visit is an excellent opportunity for a thorough, professional health check.

ANNUAL CHECKS

Even if your rabbit appears healthy, your vet will take the opportunity to examine him thoroughly when you take him for his vaccinations (see below). It is particularly important to remind your vet to check the back teeth if your rabbit is insured, as an annual dental check is a condition of most rabbit health insurance policies.

The annual vet check is an ideal time to discuss any niggling concerns you may have about your bunny's health. Some vets, particularly those in the US, recommend regular blood tests as your rabbit gets older, to pick up any developing problems as early as possible. There is no definite evidence that this approach is beneficial, but it seems logical and likely to become more widely promoted in the UK.

Early signs of illness are likely to be more easily overlooked in outdoor rabbits than indoor ones.

CHOOSING A VET

Today, it is much easier to find a 'rabbit-friendly' vet than it was a few years ago. Many urban practices have at least one vet interested in rabbits. However, rabbit medicine is still quite a specialised field and it is likely that you may have to do some research to find a veterinary practice with suitable expertise and facilities to care for your houserabbit.

To determine whether a vet is suitable, you will need to ask some questions. Do not be put off; as a potential client it is perfectly reasonable to ensure that you are satisfied with the facilities and expertise on offer. Try to choose a vet that can answer yes to all the questions on the following checklist.

• Are vaccinations for VHD and myxomatosis recommended?
• Are rabbits of both sexes routinely neutered with a good success rate?
• Has your vet invested in surgical, anaesthetic and monitoring equipment to help make surgery safer for rabbits?
• Does the practice routinely use heat pads and give warmed fluids to rabbits?
• Are pain-relieving drugs given to all rabbits after neutering operations?
• Are rabbits hospitalised away from dogs, cats, and ferrets?

If you have a choice of suitable practices within reach, you may want to consider other factors, such as the convenience of the surgery hours and the size of the practice. Some larger practices have branch surgeries with different opening hours. Large, multi-vet practices are sometimes better equipped, with round-the-clock nursing care, but it may be difficult to arrange to see the same 'rabbit-friendly' vet at each visit. Single-handed vets may not see enough rabbit patients to justify investing in lots of special equipment, but they can always refer your rabbit to a specialist if he requires surgery. A really good 'rabbit GP' is a very satisfactory solution.

Working with your vet

You will be working in partnership with your vet to keep your bunny healthy. You know your rabbit better than anyone else, but your vet has the training and expertise to interpret what you notice. Write down information to help your vet make a diagnosis. Why do you think something is wrong? When did you first notice a problem? What has happened since?

Routine visits for vaccination boosters and health checks are also opportunities to learn. Most rabbit owners have something they would like to ask and this is the perfect time to make use of your vet's expertise. Ask questions and set your mind at rest.

Occasionally, rabbits develop particularly difficult health problems, or conditions outside the area of expertise of your own vet. In these

INSURANCE MATTERS!

Good veterinary care is not cheap! Fees for a complex problem can easily run into hundreds, or even thousands, of pounds. Pet health insurance is highly recommended to cover the cost of unexpected accident or illness. Insure your rabbit as soon as possible, because pre-existing conditions will not be covered. Routine care (vaccinations, neutering, preventative dental care) is not covered and you will have to pay the first part of every claim. However, should your rabbit become seriously ill, pet insurance can, quite literally, be a lifesaver.

SAXON WARRIOR

The story of Claire King and her three-year-old French Lop, Saxon, is not only a tale of modern veterinary medicine working at its best, but also a cautionary tale in why pet insurance is such a good idea!

"Saxon has had two chronic health problems since he was 18 months old. He started off with a calcium stone blocking his ureter. This caused urine to back-flow into his kidneys, making him very ill and needing a life-saving operation to remove the stone.

"The stone removed was made of calcium, so Saxon was put on a strict, low-calcium diet. He now munches a mound of fruit and vegetables his own body size every day, and a whole bale of hay every three weeks! Despite this, he developed a second stone just three months later, which also required urgent surgery. He now has regular blood tests and X-rays to gauge his calcium status.

"Almost simultaneously with these events, a routine check-up revealed pus in Saxon's ears, and trying to cure his stubborn ear complaint has been hard work for everyone concerned. For a whole year, we tried countless eardrops, a three-month course of injectable antibiotics, and we had him sedated to have his ears flushed several times. Nothing seemed to help.

"Because treating the external ear didn't work, we thought the pus must have come from the

Saxon after ear surgery.

middle ear. An X-ray of his head was inconclusive, so Saxon's specialist recommended a CT scan, to get a definitive answer as to whether the infection really was in the middle ear or just a very stubborn external-ear infection. The CT, to everyone's surprise, revealed that the bulla part of the ear was filled with air rather than pus, just as it should be.

"Saxon had surgery on his left ear, followed by the right ear six weeks later. The surgery, known as a lateral wall resection, has not cured the problem, but makes it more manageable and his ears easier to clean. He continues to require regular trips to the vet for flushing of his ears, plus daily eardrops and cleaning performed at home.

"Needless to say, cutting-edge surgery, CT scans and specialists don't come cheap. Saxon's veterinary bills for the past two years have amounted to several thousand pounds each year. Luckily, he was insured, and his pet insurance company have been marvellous and paid the vast majority of the costs. But, even so, I ended up paying out several hundred pounds."

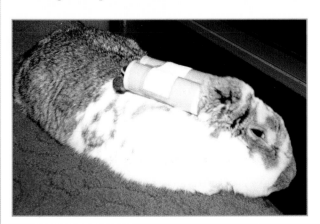

Saxon's ears have posed persistent problems, but he was a model patient throughout his treatment.

cases, a referral to a specialist may be suggested. This may be to a 'systems specialist', such as a dermatologist, neurologist or ophthalmologist. Alternatively, a second opinion may be suggested if the case is particularly baffling, or to reassure both vet and owner, or to review a chronic problem and devise a suitable management plan.

Never be afraid to ask for a second opinion. Asking your vet for a referral will not offend – it is perfectly reasonable to seek expert input in a difficult case. Everyone learns from specialist referrals and you have the reassurance of knowing you are doing everything possible to keep your rabbit healthy. All referrals must be made by your usual vet, to allow the second vet to discuss the rabbit's full medical history with the referring practitioner.

IDENTIFYING EMERGENCIES

Luckily, many health problems are not urgent, and seeing the vet within 24 to 48 hours is fine. However, if your rabbit shows any of the following danger signs, take him straight to the vet, whatever the time of day or night.
- Rabbit struggling to breathe, or lips and tongue bluish in colour.
- Rabbit limp, floppy or cold. This is a desperately ill bunny. A floppy state could indicate late-stage dehydration, shock, or overwhelming infection. The rabbit may crouch in a corner and 'feel funny' when picked up. Wrap him up warmly and get him to the vet as soon as possible.
- Uncontrollable bleeding. Bleeding that cannot be controlled by firm direct pressure applied for several minutes needs prompt veterinary attention. If your rabbit is attacked by another animal, telephone the vet for advice even if there are no obvious injuries.
- Flystrike. Maggots, usually found around the

rabbit's bottom, should be treated by the vet immediately.
- Severe diarrhoea. Bunnies who are sitting in a pool of either liquid/watery faeces or jelly-like material need immediate help. Baby rabbits are especially vulnerable to developing fatal acute diarrhoea.
- Fractured backs and legs.
- Rabbit in pain. Signs of pain in rabbits are subtle. They may sit hunched up, with their eyes half-closed, reluctant to move, sometimes grinding their teeth firmly. Ring the vet for advice. Tummy pain is the most common cause, so check the litter tray before picking up the telephone. Look for small droppings, pools of diarrhoea, or droppings strung together by strands of hair.

VACCINATION

Just like dogs and cats, rabbits need vaccinations to protect them against killer diseases. In the UK, two vaccinations are recommended for pet rabbits. These are for myxomatosis and Viral Haemorrhagic Disease commonly called VHD or HVD.

Myxomatosis has been around for many years. You may well be familiar with the distressing sight of a myxi-ravaged wild rabbit. This disease is caused by a virus, which is spread mainly by biting insects/arthropods, such as mosquitoes or fleas. Vaccination against myxomatosis should be regarded as part of a package of preventative measures. You should also discuss insect control measures with your vet.

The vaccine used to protect against myxomatosis is made from a live, but harmless, related virus called Shope Fibroma. Boosters are required every 6 to 12 months, depending on local risk and the national situation. Your vet will have information on the latest recommendation for your area.

Myxomatosis is an horrific, deadly disease, against which all pet rabbits should be vaccinated.

VHD is an appalling new disease of rabbits. It first appeared in China in 1984, reaching the UK in 1992. The first confirmed outbreak in the US occurred in spring 2000. It causes internal bleeding and kills up to 90 per cent of its victims within two to three days of infection. Strangely, baby rabbits less than eight weeks of age are not affected.

Vaccination is the only realistic method of protecting your bunny from VHD. This virus is so tough it can survive in the environment for many months, and it is highly resistant to disinfection. The VHD vaccine currently used in the UK and Australia is given every 12 months.

Although houserabbits are at lower risk from these diseases than outdoor pet rabbits, they still need to be vaccinated. VHD, in particular, is so easy to catch that it just isn't worth taking the risk. You could bring the virus home on your shoes, or it may be found in hay or food. Both vaccines have been used safely on millions of rabbits. Serious side effects are very rare,

although some rabbits are off-colour for a day or two, and there are occasional skin reactions at the injection site. These minor problems are a small price to pay for protecting your beloved rabbit from an horrific death.

Australian pet rabbits can only be vaccinated against VHD, although there is a campaign to allow myxomatosis vaccination. There are currently no rabbit vaccines available in the US.

NEUTERING

As little as ten years ago, it was unusual to have a male rabbit castrated, and having a female spayed was almost unheard of. Today, the situation has completely reversed, and small-animal veterinary surgeons are increasingly recommending the routine neutering of pet rabbits.

As we discussed earlier (see Chapter Seven), neutered rabbits make much better indoor pets. However, there are several other very good reasons why you should consider having your rabbit neutered.

Firstly, there are important health benefits, particularly for females. Up to 85 per cent of female rabbits will develop uterine cancer by the age of five unless they are spayed, and the disease can develop at a much younger age. As the operation removes the uterus and the ovaries, spayed females cannot develop this form of cancer. Similarly, castrated male rabbits can never develop testicular tumours.

The second argument in favour of neutering is behavioural. By reducing the aggressive and territorial behaviour that is driven by reproductive hormones, neutering allows pairs or groups of rabbits to live together without them fighting or breeding. This is an important benefit for a social animal like the rabbit.

Neutering involves a surgical operation. For males, the testicles are removed, either through a small incision in the scrotum, or via a single incision in the lower abdomen. Females have their ovaries and uterus removed, usually through a mid-line incision on the abdomen.

Spaying is a bigger operation than castration. However, the female rabbit has the most to gain – protection from a dangerous cancer. Male rabbits usually bounce back after their castration and come home looking for supper. Females are often quiet for a day or two, but should be eating and drinking within hours, provided they have been given sufficient pain relief.

In the past, many vets were reluctant to neuter rabbits because they experienced difficulties anaesthetising them, and the risk of death during surgery was unacceptably high. The situation is now completely different. Surgery in any animal always carries a risk, but, with modern anaesthetic techniques in experienced hands, neutering operations in rabbits are almost as safe as in cats. However, if your rabbit is over three years of age, overweight, or has other health problems (particularly a history of snuffles or related disorders), then anaesthesia and neutering carry higher risks. You should discuss the risks and benefits of neutering with a suitably experienced vet before deciding whether or not to go ahead.

Timing
Rabbits benefit from neutering at any age. Even older bucks will stop spraying and calm down after neutering. If you adopted your bunny as a youngster, you will recognise when the time is right for neutering because your cute baby bunny will suddenly become a stroppy adolescent! This usually happens around four to six months, sometimes a bit earlier in the dwarf breeds and later if your rabbit comes of age in the winter.

Up to 85 per cent of unspayed females develop uterine cancer by the age of five years.

Be guided by your vet on the best timing of the surgery. For example, some rabbit surgeons prefer to spay female rabbits just before puberty, before internal fat is laid down around the reproductive organs. Others prefer to leave it a month or two later.

If you have male and female rabbits running together, you must be especially careful not to have any accidental pregnancies. Male rabbits can be neutered as soon as their testicles descend at an age of 10 to 14 weeks. If you have your buck castrated within a day or two of this event, then he can stay with his female companion. At any later age, newly castrated rabbits can remain fertile for almost four weeks after being castrated, because mature sperm may already have left the testicle and be stored in the spermatic duct. Don't let unspayed females run with the male during this time.

If you think your female rabbit might be pregnant, it is possible to spay her in early pregnancy and remove the embryos inside the uterus. However, this carries a greater risk than spaying a rabbit who isn't pregnant, as the blood supply to the uterus greatly increases during pregnancy.

Finally, unlike dogs and cats, rabbits are unable to vomit, so they do not need to be fasted before surgery. In fact, starving a rabbit overnight can be harmful, as it will take the gut longer to get moving again post-operatively. Some vets take away food for about an hour before surgery, to try and ensure that the mouth is empty, but most offer food and water right up to the time of surgery and immediately the bunny wakes up.

NURSING CARE
It is very likely that, at some stage in your rabbit's life, you will have to care for him when he becomes sick. It is important that you try to provide him with all the conditions that will meet his behavioural and physical needs, so aiding his recovery.

Sickness
If your rabbit is ill, confine him to a cage or small area, even if he normally has free run of the house. Sick rabbits tend to sit still anyway, and a rabbit that still has a desire to run around the house is probably not desperately ill. Any rabbit feeling poorly or recovering from an anaesthetic may be wobbly on his feet and will appreciate the security of a surrogate burrow. Line the cage bottom with something soft, warm, and easily cleaned. Veterinary bedding (a synthetic fleece) is perfect, but cotton towels are also useful. Put food and water within easy reach.

The box or cage needs to be placed somewhere warm and quiet. As rabbits are small animals, they lose body heat easily. A sick rabbit needs a constantly warm environment to reduce the energy expended on keeping warm. A centrally heated home will be perfectly fine, but remember to keep the heating on at night in winter! Electrically heated pet pads are often appreciated, but remember to bunny-proof the cable. Many rabbits announce their recovery by chomping through unguarded cables. Alternatively, a hot-water bottle filled with hand-warm water and wrapped carefully in a towel can be placed next to your rabbit patient.

Post-operative care
If your rabbit has had surgery, you will need to check the wound daily. Any sign of redness or discharge should be reported to the vet. Many rabbit owners worry about rabbits unpicking their stitches, but most rabbit vets use suturing techniques that completely bury the stitches, making it virtually impossible for the rabbit to damage the wound. 'Elizabethan collars' are

If your bunny usually has free range of the home, he should be confined to a warm, quiet cage while he is recovering from illness.

only used in rabbits when absolutely essential – most rabbits hate them, and the collar also interferes with the normal process of coprophagy. After surgery, keep an eye out to ensure that your rabbit is producing droppings as normal. If not, speak to your vet.

Company

If your rabbit is one of a bonded pair, keep both bunnies together. The healthy rabbit will often groom the sick companion, and separation increases the stress to both. However, although your rabbit may appreciate the company of his rabbit companion, he is less likely to welcome contact with you. It is natural that you will want to cuddle your poorly rabbit, but most sick rabbits prefer to be left alone as much as possible.

This is because your pet bunny is genetically programmed to react to illness in just the same way as his wild cousins. He will feel vulnerable and may be frightened by things to which he is usually accustomed, such as loud noises, dogs and cats, and even his human family. So, do not impose yourself on him. You could always sit on the floor nearby, and, if he wants contact with you, he can choose to come over to you.

Fluids

One of the biggest battles when nursing very sick rabbits is persuading them to eat and drink. If a rabbit is reluctant to drink, try offering water in both a bowl and bottle. Some rabbits will drink from a bowl even when they cannot be bothered to sip from a bottle. If your bunny stops drinking completely, the situation is more serious. It is vital to get fluids in somehow, otherwise dehydration will develop rapidly, and, if not treated, lead to shock from lack of circulating fluid.

Administering fluids into the mouth by syringe is one option, but this can be stressful for both rabbit and owner. A better option, in many cases, is subcutaneous fluids. Sterile fluid is injected under the skin and absorbed directly into the bloodstream, bypassing the gut. Your vet may be willing to teach you how to do this at home. Critically ill rabbits may need to be admitted to the veterinary hospital for intravenous fluids.

Solids

Persuading sick rabbits to eat can also be difficult and frustrating. Always offer hay and your rabbit's usual favourite food. Fresh herbs in pots are often appreciated. Growing herbs, such as basil, coriander, parsley and chives, are available from supermarkets and freshly picked grass (not lawn clippings) is ideal. You may have to feed it strand by strand. If that doesn't work, try a selection of tempting, mushy foods. Microwave slices of apple till soft, and mash them up with a little sugar. Alternatively, try peeling and mashing grapes. Soften up rabbit mix with warm water, or liquidise a heap of grass and vegetables. You could also try mashed banana.

If none of these work, you will have to force-feed by syringe. Special convalescent diets, designed to be syringe-fed, are available, and it is worth keeping a packet in stock for emergencies. If nothing else is available, cereal-based baby food can be used, although foods rich in sugar and starch are not normally recommended. However, if the gut has nothing to work with, it will shut down entirely, so it is better to get something into the bunny than nothing at all.

Cleanliness

Although sick rabbits do not appreciate fuss, they don't like to be dirty. If your rabbit is one of a bonded pair, the mate will usually clean away eye and nasal discharge, but if you have only one bunny, this will be your job. If the eyes are running badly, clipping away the wet, matted fur on the face will make it much easier to clean and help to prevent chapping of the skin. Similarly, rabbits with severe diarrhoea or urine scald will be much easier to nurse if you carefully clip away the soiled fur. The skin of the inner hind legs, tummy and genital region is extremely easy to cut, so be careful.

ADMINISTERING MEDICATION

Administering medication to rabbits is not easy. To start with, you can try to disguise oral medicine in something tasty. Put it on to a piece of banana, or smear on to a slice of apple that's been scored lots of times with a knife. Unfortunately, rabbits aren't daft and many antibiotics are pretty horrible to taste, so it is often necessary to give medicines by syringe.

Using a syringe

If you have to give your rabbit medicine, fluid or food via syringe, the priority is to prevent injury to you or to the bunny. It is a good idea to ask your vet to demonstrate some handling techniques. Most people wrap the rabbit tightly in a towel, including the front paws, leaving only the head free. You can then sit the rabbit on your lap, facing away from you, and lean over him; or put him on the floor and crouch over him; or turn him upside down, tucking his body under your left armpit, parting his lips with your left hand and using your right hand to manipulate the syringe.

Rabbits have a gap between the incisor teeth and the molars, and this is where you insert the nozzle of the syringe. Make sure the needle is removed. In theory, all you have to do is gently

A pair of rabbits will groom each other – something you must do instead if you keep a single bunny.

wriggle the syringe behind the incisors and squirt the medicine on to the tongue. In practice, the rabbit will often spit out or refuse to swallow foul-tasting drugs. If the rabbit is well enough to put up a good fight, some people resort to smearing the medicine round the bunny's lips so he will lick it off.

Giving drops

Eye and eardrops are usually much easier to adminster, and you may not have to wrap the rabbit in a towel. Eardrops are put into the base of the ear, and you must massage the medication deep into the ear canal before the rabbit vigorously shakes his head.

To give eyedrops, gently turn back the lower eyelid and put the medicine into the pocket so formed. To adminster eye ointment, you will need to squirt a 1-cm (about a half-an-inch) strand of ointment into the eye. You'll find it easier to achieve this if you store eye ointment in the fridge.

SAYING GOODBYE

As your rabbit enters his senior years, you will become more aware of the fact that, sooner or later, you will have to say goodbye. Old rabbits, not infrequently, go into a long, slow decline, developing a series of problems that become increasingly difficult to control. When the bad days outnumber the good, or when your bunny shows no sign of enjoying his favourite treats, then it may be time to let him go. Hopefully, by the time your rabbit's life draws to a close, you will have a trusting relationship with your vet, and you can discuss the option of euthanasia together.

Sometimes it is obvious that euthanasia is the only humane option, but sometimes it is difficult to know when to let go. Rabbits are sensitive to the moods of their carers, and, if

you are becoming distressed caring for a terminally ill animal, then it is not fair on either of you to prolong things. Similarly, you may find yourself with work or domestic responsibilities that make it impossible for you to provide the care necessary to maintain your rabbit's quality of life. In this situation, you must not feel guilty about reaching the decision that euthanasia is the kindest option for the rabbit you love.

Euthanasia is usually carried out by lethal injection; it is literally an overdose of anaesthetic. Your rabbit will feel no more than the prick of a needle. Some vets give a sedative injection first, relaxing the rabbit and enabling the actual euthanasia injection to be given directly into a vein. Alternatively, the injection may be given directly into the lungs, heart or kidneys. It is worth asking your vet which method is preferred, so that you can be mentally prepared. You may or may not wish to stay with your rabbit at this time. Whatever you decide, it is often comforting to spend some time with the body afterwards and give your bunny a last cuddle.

Coping with the death of a beloved pet is not easy. Houserabbits become just as much a part of the family as dogs and cats, and the grief and sense of loss we experience on their death is intense and deeply distressing. Sadly, few people understand just how special the human/rabbit bond can be, so many bereaved houserabbit owners find little understanding from family and colleagues.

Marking the passing of your bunny in some special way can help the grieving process. If you have a garden, you may want to bury your bunny, perhaps under a favourite bush. If this is not possible, or you know you are likely to move house in the future, then consider a pet graveyard or a cremation. You can choose to have your pet cremated individually, in which case the ashes will be returned to you. Some people like to keep the ashes; others scatter them somewhere meaningful and peaceful.

There are several avenues of support available for bereaved pet owners. The Society for Companion Animal Studies runs a Pet Bereavement Hotline in the UK. In the US, some veterinary schools organise pet bereavement counselling run by their veterinary students.

The national houserabbit associations (RWA and HRS) are also experienced in supporting those grieving the loss of their rabbit companion. Don't feel you have to struggle through this difficult time alone.

LETTING GO

Sally Walshaw, herself a respected rabbit vet from the US, describes the painful process of deciding to euthanase Larry, her own much-loved houserabbit.

"Letting go of a beloved rabbit is very difficult. It takes courage and love to choose euthanasia. However, when the rabbit is having more bad days than good days, and more painful moments than happy moments, the owner has to make a very difficult decision. A rabbit in pain may be more afraid than we can imagine. In nature, rabbits are prey animals, and they rely on escape to avoid injury.

"A diagnosis of a painful fatal illness has been the reason for euthanasia of several of my rabbits over the past 30 years. Larry was a 10–year-old New Zealand rabbit that developed multicentric lymphosarcoma. The oncologist said his disease was too advanced to treat with chemotherapy. Larry began losing weight, and, ultimately, the cancer in his lungs caused difficulty breathing.

"On the day I chose for euthanasia, I set aside a large amount of time with Larry, to talk to him and to offer some special treats. Larry loved breakfast cereal and he ate an entire bowl of it while I told some funny stories, reminding him about the good times.

"Just prior to the euthanasia, while holding Larry, I imagined the perfect situation for this dear rabbit. I imagined him exploring an interesting room and chewing on lots of stuff like boxes and magazines and finding secret treasure troves of Cheerios. These mental pictures helped me to keep calm. The goal of euthanasia is a peaceful death. (I had cried before my last long session with Larry, and I wept after the euthanasia session, but I did not want to upset Larry by crying during the actual procedure.)

"Larry received a sedative injected under the skin and then I waited about 10 minutes for that to take effect. Then the euthanasia solution was administered intravenously. Then I cried and told myself that this beautiful rabbit deserved to have someone who mourned his passing. I tried to remember that all the tears would never take away all the joy and all the things that Larry taught me through the years. Sadness is not something to be feared; it indicates that you have the capacity to love. It is a part of life. The fact that I am crying as I write this just means that Larry will always be present in my heart."

CHAPTER TWELVE

NOSE-TO-TAIL HEALTH GUIDE

Rabbits are susceptible to very different health problems from dogs and cats, and they present in a very different way. To help you decide when your rabbit is ill, you need to be able to recognise normality. This nose-to-tail guide will take you through what you can expect to see in a normal, healthy rabbit, as well as background information about some of the more common problems associated with each body system.

THE NOSE

Normal
Your rabbit's nose should be clean and dry. Some condensation may be visible around the nostrils if your rabbit plays outside in cold weather. Breathing should be quiet. Some breeds with round heads and flat faces make 'snuffling' noises while eating. This may be normal as long as there is no nasal discharge present. The odd sneeze due to transient irritation from dust is nothing to worry about.

Warning signs
- Sneezing
- Nasal discharge
- Noisy or 'rattly' breathing
- Matted fur on the inner surface of the front paws.

If your rabbit is sneezing repeatedly, or has developed a runny nose, there is a problem. Check the fur on the inner surface of the front paws to confirm the presence of a discharge. Rabbits use their paws as handkerchiefs, and matted, wet fur here may be the only visible sign of a significant nasal discharge.

'Snuffles'
This is an informal term used to describe a sneezing rabbit with a runny nose. Possible causes of these signs include a foreign body in the nose, teeth/eye problems, or even tumours, particularly if the discharge is from only one nostril. However, 'snuffles' usually refers to a bacterial infection in the upper respiratory tract.

The rabbit's nose should be dry and clean.

While the usual cause of 'snuffles' is a bacterium called *Pasteurella multocida*, this is not the only possible culprit. The only way to be sure is for your vet to perform a culture-and-sensitivity (c-and-s) test on a swab taken from deep inside the nose. This will enable the vet to determine what species of bacteria is causing the problem and which antibiotic is the best choice of treatment.

Pasteurella

This bacterium is a particular problem for rabbits. The majority of rabbits have it living in their noses and throats quite harmlessly. However, if the population of *Pasteurella* bacteria suddenly increases, disease may occur. Treatment aims to reduce the infection to a level at which the rabbit's own immune system can take over and keep the bacterial population in check once again. An appropriate antibiotic is needed in an adequate dose for a suitable period of time. This may be several weeks or considerably longer. Some rabbits may even require antibiotics for life. Symptoms may flare up again if the rabbit is stressed or if the

immune system is depressed in any way. A history of snuffles is a risk marker for other *Pasteurella*-related problems, such as abscesses and pneumonia.

Rabbits have sensitive noses. A dry, dusty atmosphere may predispose them to problems and smoking is likely to be particularly irritating. If you are a smoker, try not to smoke in the presence of your rabbit.

THE EYES

Normal

Healthy rabbits have bright, clear eyes. There should be no discharge. Some rabbits (particularly giant breeds) have a prominent third eyelid. Loose hairs on the front of their eye can look remarkably like a dramatic scratch, but this will disappear when the rabbit blinks.

Warning signs

• Runny eyes
• Red, sore-looking eyes
• Matted facial fur
• A single bulging eye
• A hazy appearance on the eye
• Swelling around the eyes and face
• Fur loss below the eye
• Matted fur on the legs.

Any change in the appearance of the eye is abnormal. If your rabbit has a slight runny eye, you could try bathing it with cooled boiled water. If the problem persists for more than 12 to 24 hours, the rabbit will need to see the vet. Conjunctivitis is common, but it is easily treated with antibiotic eye ointment or drops. Scratched eyes (corneal abrasions) are another common cause of a runny eye. The treatment is the same – antibiotics until the scratch heals over. The rabbit should return to normal within a few days.

Round-headed breeds, such as the Netherland Dwarf (pictured), are prone to blocked tear ducts.

If, despite treatment, the runny eye persists, there may be a more serious problem. For example, the tear duct may be blocked. This is a particular problem in round-headed breeds, such as Lops and Netherland Dwarfs. Blocked and infected tear ducts (dacrocystitis) can be linked to serious dental disease, if the upper teeth have overgrown to an extent where they impinge on the tear duct. A full diagnosis will require further tests. If your rabbit has a runny eye that is not quickly cured by simple treatment, your vet is likely to recommend sedating or anaesthetising the rabbit to examine him thoroughly. This will enable a skull X-ray to be taken, to assess the state of the tear ducts and teeth. The tear ducts can be flushed at the same time.

Another cause of running or irritated eyes is entropion, where the eyelids turn inwards and the eyelashes scratch the eyes, a condition which requires surgical correction. Myxomatosis causes

swelling around the eyes and genital regions and sometimes conjunctivitis.

Odd-looking eyes are sometimes seen both with cataracts (when the pupil becomes white) and glaucoma (when raised pressure within the eye causes the eye to get bigger, sometimes accompanied by a hazy blue cornea). Both these conditions may be hereditary, and glaucoma needs prompt veterinary attention. Much more rare is lens rupture, caused by a parasite called *Encephalitzoon cuniculi*.

THE MOUTH

Normal
The fur around your rabbit's mouth should be dry, with no signs of dribbling or drooling. The teeth should not be overgrown and they should never protrude beyond the lips. The front teeth should be checked at home (see Chapter Four).

Warning signs
• A hungry rabbit that seems reluctant to eat
• Weight loss
• Change in preferred foods
• Drooling
• Wet chin or dewlap
• Lumps along the lower jaw
• Teeth protruding from the mouth
• Tender jaw
• Persistently runny eyes.

Dental disease
Dental disease is extremely common in pet rabbits, and it can develop at any age. It is also potentially serious, so any hint of a problem merits a trip to the vet. Rabbits are designed to spend a lot of time chewing grass, using their back teeth to grind the strands of vegetation. Grass is an abrasive substance that helps to wear the continuously growing teeth to the correct

length. Problems may develop if the crowns grow too long. If the teeth then have no space to grow upwards, they will grow backwards instead, forcing the tooth roots too far down into the jaw. This weakens the bone and triggers a chain of problems, which may culminate in infection and abscess formation around the jaw. Also, sharp spurs or ridges may develop on the back teeth, which can lead to painful lesions on the tongue and cheeks.

It is still not entirely clear exactly what causes dental disease in rabbits, but a number of factors are implicated.

- **Diet:** a major factor affecting dental health. Veterinary surgeons are not certain whether the problem is due to food texture (lack of chewing action results in a failure of normal tooth wear), a deficiency of calcium, or both. The most important point to remember is that a healthy, grass/hay-based diet contains sufficient calcium as well as providing suitable material to maintain correct mouth mechanics.
- **Breed:** although dental disease is common in all rabbits, Lops and Netherland Dwarfs seem particularly vulnerable. As well as molar teeth problems, these breeds are at risk of hereditary incisor malocclusion. This can become apparent as early as 6 to 12 weeks of age or as late as 12-18 months, when skeletal development is complete.
- **Trauma:** if a rabbit breaks a tooth, the opposite tooth will grow unopposed. This problem is usually seen with the incisors.
- **Age:** 'spurs' on molar teeth are common in older rabbits. There is some controversy about whether these are normal in older rabbits or whether they reflect an underlying disruption in dental wear and mechanics.
- **Infection:** these are a disaster for rabbits. Tooth-root infections may progress to

Rabbits are designed to chew grass for much of the day – an action that keeps the teeth to the correct length.

abscesses or infection of the actual jaw bone (osteomyelitis), all of which carry a very poor prognosis.

There are several steps you can take to try to reduce the chances of your bunny developing dental problems. Most important is a diet based on grass or hay, mimicking that of a wild rabbit. A properly balanced diet does not require any vitamin or calcium supplements – too much calcium is as harmful as too little.

Try not to choose a high-risk breed. If your heart is set on a Lop or Netherland Dwarf, either adopt an adult rescue that has had a dental check at the time of neutering, or obtain a youngster from a reputable breeder whose rabbits have no history of teeth problems. Think carefully before taking on a rabbit with known dental problems. They can be heartbreaking as well as costly, and pre-existing conditions are usually excluded from pet insurance policies.

Finally, have your rabbit's teeth checked regularly. A quick look with an auroscope when your bunny sees the vet for vaccinations may pick up some problems. However, if the rabbit develops signs suggesting dental disease, a more thorough examination will be required. This usually entails anaesthetising or sedating the rabbit, so the vet can examine the mouth and tongue, and taking X-rays of the skull and jaws.

Overgrown teeth

Overgrown incisor teeth can be shortened to the correct length every few weeks; or removed altogether. Although this entails an operation, it offers a permanent solution and it is increasingly recommended by rabbit vets. In contrast, clipping teeth is rapidly falling out of favour, and most vets now use a dental burr instead.

Spurs on the molar teeth may require filing, or the height of the back teeth crowns may be reduced with a dental burr to restore the correct bite. Some rabbits get away with just one or two treatments for mild problems, but the majority require repeated treatment.

Rabbits undergoing dental treatment are often high-risk patients for surgery. They may be malnourished if they haven't eaten properly for some time, or dehydrated if a sore mouth has made them reluctant to drink. Your vet may suggest admitting the rabbit for fluid therapy and observation beforehand. Post-operative pain relief is required after most dental procedures, to enable the rabbit to eat comfortably.

THE EARS

Normal

The ears should be clean and dry, free from lumps, swellings or discharge.

Warning signs
- Shaking the head
- Scratching at the ears
- Visible ear wax
- Smelly ears
- Head tilted to one side
- Rabbit resents ears being touched.

Rabbits have large ears that are highly mobile (except in Lop breeds), enabling the rabbit to listen carefully for any signs of danger. Fortunately, ear problems are not particularly common, even among Lop breeds.

Ear mites

Ear mites are sometimes seen, especially in rescued animals, producing a condition known as canker. The mites invade the ear canal, causing intense irritation and triggering production of a crusty discharge from one or

The ears should be clean and fresh-smelling.

both ears. The first signs are subtle. You may notice your bunny scratching his ears, or that the base of the ear is sore when touched. Within two weeks, there will be an obvious grey-brown scaly crust within the ear itself. If left untreated, mites and exudate spill out on to the cheeks and neck. This looks as disgusting as it sounds.

Ear mites require treatment by a vet, which normally consists of injections of ivermectin to kill the mites, plus topical applications to soften the exudate. Some newer strategies are being investigated. Anti-inflammatory drugs may also be used, partly for pain relief. Antibiotics are sometimes required to control secondary bacterial infection. These may be used either topically (directly to the ear), or systemically (by injection or orally). Occasionally, the crusts are so painful that the rabbit will need a few days of treatment to soften the crusts, followed by a general anaesthetic to allow removal of them.

Head tilt

This is also known as 'torticollis' or 'wry neck'. The rabbit's head twists over to one side, and the bunny may fall over repeatedly. This condition has several possible causes, ranging from a bacterial inner ear infection (usually *Pasteurella*, sometimes *Pseudomonas* or other bugs) to a brain parasite called *E. cuniculi*. It may also be caused by a stroke or meningitis.

Treatment may consist of antibiotics, anti-inflammatories, steroids, or anti-parasitic drugs (to try and kill off *E.cuniculi*), depending on which the vet feels is the most likely cause.

Torticollis can be a stubborn and difficult problem to treat, and it tends to recur. Careful nursing is essential, and anecdotal reports from the US suggest that complementary therapies (e.g. acupuncture) may be helpful. Head tilt can be distressing – severely affected rabbits may be unable to stand up. If a rabbit with torticollis

does not respond to treatment, and cannot eat or move without assistance, euthanasia may be the kindest option.

THE SKIN

Normal

Healthy rabbits should have a shiny coat, free of parasites. There should be regular periods of moulting when the coat is replaced. A small, pink, callused area on the point of the hock is normal.

Warning signs

- Dandruff or scurf
- Scratching
- Sore or bare patches in the fur
- Lumps and bumps
- Maggots
- Unpleasant smells
- Red or raw areas on the point of the hock, or on the pads of the feet.

The coat is a good indicator of general health.

Moult

The most commonly observed 'skin problem' is actually a normal moult. All rabbits have slightly different moult patterns. Some will moult fully and rapidly twice a year, while others shed their coat continuously. The latter is especially true of thick-coated rabbits living in a centrally heated home.

Moulting can be very dramatic, with tufts of fur falling out. You may see a temporary pigmentation of skin in the moulting area, a 'tide-mark' where the new fur is growing through, or an area of short coat like a Rex rabbit. All are quite normal. Moulting rabbits need frequent grooming, which will reduce the chance of hair blocking up either your rabbit's gut or your vacuum cleaner.

Mites

As you groom your rabbit, look carefully for any dandruff, particularly behind the ears and along the spine. Scurf or dandruff indicates a mite infestation. This is most often due to a species called *Cheyletiella*. This common problem is now usually treated with three injections of ivermectin, given seven to ten days apart. This treatment has largely replaced medicated shampoos, much to the relief of many rabbits and their owners. Some newer anti-parasitic preparations are under investigation and will hopefully make treatment even more simple and effective in the near future. Mites can survive away from the rabbit, so bedding and cages must be carefully cleaned. Incidentally, *Cheyletiella* can also affect humans and cause a mild itchy rash that disappears when the rabbit has been treated.

Ringworm

Another condition that can affect both rabbits and humans (and other domestic pets) is the fungal infection ringworm. This appears as bare patches or sores on rabbits, and round, scaly patches on humans. All affected parties require treatment.

Wounds

If you keep a group of rabbits, occasional squabbles are almost inevitable. Luckily, the resultant wounds are usually minor. Clean wounds with saline solution (a teaspoonful of salt to a pint of water), and carefully inspect the wound. If it is large, gaping, it won't stop bleeding, or if it involves a structure such as an eyelid, the rabbit needs prompt veterinary attention.

Abscesses

Abscesses are serious. These collections of pus, surrounded by a thick, fibrous wall, may develop after a bite or other wound. They are also found around the mouth, due to dental disease.

Treatment aims to remove the entire abscess, including the wall. Sometimes, this is simply not possible and the vet may have to settle for draining the pus, followed by one of a variety of strategies to try and kill off any residual bugs. Antibiotic-impregnated beads, glucose paste, and commercial gels are all under investigation. With intensive nursing and wound care, combined with rational use of surgery and antibiotics, the outlook for rabbits with abscesses is improving. However, they can be a recurrent and long-term problem.

Myxomatosis

The deadly viral disease myxomatosis may cause lumps to appear in the skin. Other early signs of myxomatosis include swellings around the eyes, ears, and genitalia. All pet rabbits should be vaccinated.

All rabbits can contract flystrike, but long-coated breeds are among the most vulnerable.

Flystrike

Flystrike occurs if blowflies lay eggs on wet or dirty skin and the eggs hatch into maggots. This disgusting condition is not uncommon in summer. Older, obese rabbits are particularly at risk, but long-coated animals are also vulnerable. Flystrike can develop in a matter of hours, so it is important to check rabbits frequently in warm weather. A recent development in flystrike prevention is the use of chemicals (applied as a liquid to the rabbit's bottom) that prevent fly eggs from developing into maggots.

The maggots of some fly species can eat their way deep into normal tissue, releasing toxins and making the rabbit desperately ill. Immediate treatment is vital – a badly fly-blown rabbit will be lucky to survive even with intensive therapy. Prevention is better than cure, so perform daily bottom checks, keep older rabbits well groomed and at their correct weight, and keep litter trays and hutches clean.

Sore hocks

Sore hocks – pododermatitis – was once thought to occur only in rabbits kept in dirty, damp hutches with inadequate bedding. This is only partially true, because houserabbits can develop sore hocks too. Overweight rabbits are at greater risk of developing the condition, and, if the nails grow too long, the rabbit will throw more weight on to his heels, exacerbating the problem. Rex rabbits have thinner fur on their feet and are also at higher risk, as are older, less-mobile bunnies with arthritis.

Houserabbits can get carpet burns on their front paws from leaping off furniture on to synthetic carpets. If the skin on the foot is just a little red, you may get away with changing the surface your rabbit spends most time upon. Synthetic, fur-fleece veterinary bedding is a popular option. You will also need to clip the claws and to ensure your rabbit isn't too fat! However, if this fails to work, if the skin is broken, or if there is any sign of infection, your rabbit must be treated by the vet. Successful treatment of pododermatitis may take time and ingenuity, and specialist referral is sometimes beneficial for severely affected rabbits.

Sore hocks are not exclusive to hutch-kept rabbits – houserabbits can get them from carpet burns.

THE LUNGS

Normal
The lips and the tongue should be a healthy, pink colour. Healthy rabbits should breathe fairly quietly, even after exertion. Rapid breathing is normal if the rabbit is stressed or hot.

Warning signs
• Laboured, deep breaths
• Bluish-coloured tongue and lips
• Bloody discharge from the nose
• Noisy, rattly breathing.

Any signs of respiratory distress indicate a very seriously ill rabbit and demand immediate veterinary attention. They do not necessarily indicate a lung problem, as any very sick rabbit may develop respiratory difficulty. For example, rabbits with acute gut problems may have difficulty breathing.

Pneumonia
This lung infection is probably the most common of the serious respiratory diseases. It may follow an uncontrolled bout of 'snuffles', but it may develop very suddenly, with no warning. Pneumonia can be fatal. Seriously affected rabbits need oxygen, antibiotics and very intensive treatment to stand any chance of survival.

Viral Haemorrhagic Disease
Deadlier still is Viral Haemorrhagic Disease (VHD or HVD), which first appeared in the UK in 1992 and the US in 2000. Sometimes described as 'Rabbit Ebola', VHD causes internal bleeding and liver failure, and it has killed millions of rabbits across the world. It is extremely difficult to prevent domestic rabbits from coming into contact with the virus.

However, thankfully, rabbits in most countries can now be protected by a safe and effective vaccine. It is essential that all pet rabbits are immunised every year.

Cancer
Cancer that spreads (metastasises) to the lung can be the cause of respiratory problems. The most common cancer behaving like this is uterine cancer, which is extremely common in unspayed, older female rabbits. Once the cancer has spread to the lungs, the prognosis is hopeless. This condition is preventable if you have your young female rabbit spayed.

THE SPINE & LIMBS

Normal
Rabbits should move freely, without limping. They should be flexible enough to be able to reach right round to groom their back end, and to reach the anus to ingest caecotrophs. Older rabbits are a little stiffer, and may not be able to reach their extremities so easily. It is not abnormal for young rabbits to revert to crawling one foot at a time rather than hopping, especially if they are nervous.

Warning signs
• Limping
• Inability to move the hind limbs
• Urinary incontinence
• Loss of muscle bulk in hind limbs
• Poor balance
• Caecotrophs sticking to bottom
• Unkempt fur around bottom and tail.

Wild rabbits rarely live long enough for degenerative changes to occur in their bones, but domestic rabbits frequently become a bit stiff and arthritic in old age. With rabbits increasingly being kept as companion animals, there is a growing interest in helping these older bunnies. Some benefit from long-term painkillers and anti-inflammatories, while others may benefit from gentle physiotherapy or even acupuncture.

Rabbits confined in hutches are relatively immobile, and, as a result, they can develop osteoporosis and arthritis of the spine at an early age. This can cause painful pinching of the nerves running out of the spinal cord. Houserabbits fare better, as they tend to get plenty of exercise and usually stay active even into old age.

Nevertheless, you should be prepared to help your older rabbit clean the tricky bits, such as the tummy, the vent area, and around the rump and tail. Some large and giant rabbits can develop severe and progressive hind-limb weakness as they get older, giving similar problems to those of spinally injured rabbits. Obesity is also a serious problem in older rabbits, which makes poor mobility even worse, so do not let your rabbit run to fat in his old age.

Spinal fractures may occur if the rabbit kicks out violently on being picked up, or if he is dropped. Rabbits have large, strong muscles that are actually stronger than their lightweight bones. It is vital to ensure you pick up your rabbit securely and safely, and young children should never be allowed to pick up a rabbit unsupervised. Spinal fractures may damage the spinal cord, causing hind-limb paralysis with incontinence. If your rabbit sustains such an injury, the prognosis is guarded. Cage rest, painkillers and steroids are worth a try, but if there is no improvement in two weeks, recovery is unlikely and euthanasia is usually advised.

It is possible to keep a paralysed rabbit, but the intense, time-consuming level of nursing

The rabbit should be flexible enough to groom without difficulty.

care required is simply not feasible for many rabbit owners. However, if you are determined to give it a try, your national houserabbit organisation may be able to put you in touch with an owner in a similar position for practical advice and support.

THE GUT

Normal
The best indicator of the health of your bunny's digestive system is the litter tray. Take a quick look in the tray every day, to check that your rabbit is passing the same quantity and type of droppings as is usual for him.

Warning signs
- Loss of appetite
- Small, hard droppings
- Absence of droppings
- Diarrhoea or mucus

- Rabbit sitting hunched and quiet
- Slow teeth grinding (indicates pain).

If your rabbit enjoys a suitable diet based upon grass and hay, the gut should basically take care of itself. However, occasional malfunctions can occur, usually because of some dietary disruption or indiscretion. There is a whole host of different diseases and syndromes that can affect rabbit guts, but most of them are of little relevance to houserabbits. Your job as a caring houserabbit owner is to understand how to keep the guts healthy, and to recognise problems if they occur.

Gut flora

Healthy digestion depends upon normal movement of food substrate through the gut, and a healthy population of friendly bacteria (known as gut flora) in the hind gut. Any disturbance in either of these two factors can lead to disease.

Sudden changes in diet can play havoc with gut flora, allowing the pathogenic bacteria, which cause disease, to overgrow. This can have serious, and sometimes fatal, consequences if diarrhoea develops. Newly weaned rabbits are particularly vulnerable to disruption of their gut flora. Stress or sudden dietary changes may

prove catastrophic. Young rabbits purchased from pet shops are at particular risk of fatal digestive upsets, as they have to cope with two changes of diet and environment in quick succession.

True diarrhoea is liquid or watery faeces, not just a few sloppy droppings. Any rabbit suffering from diarrhoea, who is not bright and alert, must be taken to the vet immediately. It does not take much to dehydrate a rabbit and a bunny with diarrhoea who is sitting quietly in the corner may be dying, so do not delay if you are in any doubt. Passing mucus from the rectum is a particularly ominous sign, particularly in young rabbits, and again demands urgent veterinary attention.

GI stasis

Equally worrying is when the rabbit stops eating. A bunny that is just a little bit subdued in behaviour, and whose droppings have become small and dry, is a cause for concern. This may be a sign of gastrointestinal ileus or 'GI stasis'. This slowing of the digestive tract often occurs in rabbits who are under the weather for another reason, such as pain from a dental problem or a hidden infection. It was once thought that this condition was due to furballs, because hair is sometimes found in the stomachs of these rabbits and the condition is not uncommonly seen in moulting rabbits. In actual fact, what probably happens is that the gut slows down and allows hair to accumulate in the gut rather than the other way round. Treatment is directed at getting the gut moving, rather than removing the hairball.

Most gut problems demand a similar approach to treatment. The bunny will need lots of fluid, often injected subcutaneously (under the skin) or even intravenously (into the vein). Painkillers and drugs to encourage the gut to start moving again, plus plenty of hay or other high-fibre food, should also be provided. The vet will need to search for and treat any specific underlying cause or associated problems.

Surgery is rarely required, except in the very rare cases where the gut has become totally obstructed. Dried, whole corn pips and peas from rabbit mixes have both been implicated. A rabbit with an intestinal blockage would become dramatically and suddenly ill, and their only hope of survival is a prompt operation.

THE URINARY SYSTEM

Normal

Rabbit urine varies in colour. It may be clear, yellow, orange, red, or even a thick, chalky white. The colour depends on what vegetable pigments your rabbit has been eating. Spraying of urine, particularly in un-neutered males, is not uncommon. A rabbit whose routine or territory has been disrupted (for instance by the introduction of a new rabbit or moving house) may have a temporary lapse in litter-training and urinate outside his litter box.

Warning signs
- Rabbit quiet and subdued
- Straining in the litter box
- Blood mixed with urine
- Teeth grinding
- Previously litter-trained rabbit starts to dribble urine outside litter tray for no apparent reason
- Urine-staining inside back legs.

The urinary tract consists of the kidneys, ureters, bladder and urethra. The two most common problems in this department are infections and stones (urolithiasis).

Rabbits are particularly prone to urinary stones because of the unique way they handle dietary calcium. Most mammals will only absorb the amount of calcium required by the body, but rabbits absorb calcium in proportion to what is present in the diet. Any excess calcium has to be excreted via the kidneys, and there is a limit to how much calcium can be dissolved in urine. If this limit is exceeded, the calcium will precipitate out, when it may form either discrete stones or sludge.

The rabbit's urine should be monitored every day.

Although it can be normal for a rabbit to pass red urine (particularly if they have been eating beetroot or carrots), if your rabbit has never done it before, have a urine sample tested to confirm that it isn't blood. Bear in mind that, if your rabbit is an unspayed female, the most common cause of blood in the urine is uterine cancer (see below).

If your rabbit develops any signs of urinary tract problems, the vet will need a sample of urine to test for blood, bacteria or crystals/stones. The easiest way of getting a urine sample from a houserabbit is to scrub and scald out a litter tray and wait for the bunny to urinate in it. If this doesn't work, your vet may try other tactics, such as gentle pressure on the lower abdomen. He may pass a small needle into the bladder from the outside, or pass a catheter into the bladder. This usually requires sedation or a general anaesthetic, but, as an X-ray may be needed to determine whether the rabbit has urolithiasis, it can be done at the same time.

Treatment of urinary infections is fairly simple. Antibiotics, plus whatever supportive care is required if the bunny is generally unwell, are usually sufficient. Urolithiasis is a bit more of a problem. Large stones may need to be removed surgically, and bladder sludge may need to be coaxed out. Any associated infection will require antibiotics. It is important to modify the diet, to reduce the amount of calcium absorbed by the bunny. You should also encourage your rabbit to drink more.

As your rabbit gets older, watch out for urine splashing back on to the hind legs. This sometimes occurs if the bunny is urinating on to a non-absorbent surface, but more often it is because an older bunny is getting a bit too stiff to take up the normal crouching position to urinate. Put fat rabbits on a weight-reduction diet and change to a highly absorbent litter-tray substrate. Talk to your vet about long-term painkillers for achy old bunnies.

GENITALIA

Normal
In the male rabbit, the testicles descend into the scrotum at 12 to 14 weeks of age and can be seen as surprisingly large, sausage-shaped swellings in a pinky sac at either side of the vent.

Rabbits can retract their testicles right up into the abdomen. Unspayed female rabbits usually become moody, territorial, and sometimes aggressive, during what would be the breeding season (spring through to autumn). The vulva sometimes becomes pinky-red at this time, rather than the usual pale pink.

Warning signs
• Swellings in the genital region
• Dirty, wet fur
• Wounds or signs of bleeding
• Bad smells from the back end
• Blood mixed with urine.

Houserabbits of both sexes are usually neutered as soon as they reach puberty, so problems with the reproductive tract are very rare. If you have adopted an older rabbit, or if you haven't had your rabbit neutered, you need to be aware of the potential problems.

Uterine cancer
The biggest problem for unspayed females is uterine cancer. This affects up to 85 per cent of female rabbits by the age of five years, and it is a leading cause of premature death. Because of this, we recommend that all female rabbits not intended for breeding should be spayed. If you

Houserabbits are healthier and happier than their hutched cousins.

have an unspayed doe, watch out for drops of blood in the urine at the end of urination, a pot-bellied appearance, or general loss in condition.

Sometimes, uterine cancer shows up only when the tumour has spread to the lungs, and, by this stage, euthanasia is the only option. An emergency spay is possible if the problem is recognised early enough. Uterine infections can present in a similar way.

Testicular problems

Male rabbits left uncastrated can sometimes develop testicular tumours, but trauma is probably the most common testicular problem. If entire male rabbits fight, they will often try to castrate each other using their back claws. Neutering is recommended for all male pet rabbits because it will prevent all these problems, as well as freeing the rabbit from a life sentence of solitary confinement.

Swellings

Swellings around the genitalia may indicate the early stages of myxomatosis. Check for any other signs of the disease, such as conjunctivitis, and see your vet promptly. Sores or crusts on the genitalia may suggest either pox-virus

infection or rabbit syphilis, both of which can be associated with lesions on the lips and nose. Humans cannot catch rabbit syphilis, which is usually treated by injections of penicillin. This is one of the few conditions for which rabbits are given penicillin, as it is very dangerous for them if given by mouth.

Fertility

Never forget that rabbits become fertile at a remarkably early age. If you buy two bunnies from the same litter, you will need to check the male daily from 10 to 12 weeks onwards, having him neutered as soon as the testicles descend – otherwise, you'll have a litter of babies on the way before you know it!

SUMMARY

With good preventative care and lots of love, many houserabbits live to a very respectable age, giving their owners years of friendship. Certainly, by keeping a houserabbit, you will be giving your bunny a far happier, healthier, and more fulfilled life than one mainly confined in a hutch. And, once you've been bitten by the houserabbit bug, it is very hard to contemplate life without one.